The Prince

-NICCOLO MACHIAVELLI

Writers of the Round Table Press

Executive Editor
COREY MICHAEL BLAKE

Art Direction by
NATHAN BROWN

ROUND TABLE COMICS

MACHIAVELLI

The Prince

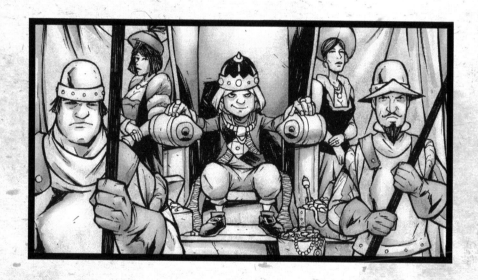

Adapted and Illustrated by

SHANE
CLESTER

IT MAY BE ANSWERED
THAT ONE SHOULD WISH TO BE
'BOTH, BUT IT IS MUCH SAFER
TO BE FEARED THAN LOVED.'

© 2011 WRITERS OF THE ROUND TABLE PRESS
ROUND TABLE COMICS

@RTCOMPANIES
WWW.ROUNDTABLECOMICS.COM

ROUND TABLE COMPANIES
PO BOX 511
HIGHLAND PARK, IL 60035
USA

PHONE: 815-346-2398

FIRST EDITION: OCTOBER 2011
ISBN: 9781610660167

"A PRINCE NEVER LACKS LEGITIMATE
REASONS TO BREAK HIS PROMISE."
- NICCOLO MACHIAVELLI

INTRODUCTION BY SHANE CLESTER

"It's better to be feared than loved."

That phrase is about all I knew about Machiavelli's *The Prince* when I first started to adapt it into this comic. Every once in awhile, someone would throw around the phrase "Machiavellian" when a person would concoct some elaborate scheme to advance his or her station in life. While I understood the intent, I didn't really know the meaning. And I thought, how relevant could philosophies from the 1500s be, anyway?

Turns out they're just as relevant today. Machiavelli's advice for "Princes" from the 1500s is just as applicable to leaders and those who hold any sort of power today. The examples he cites to illustrate his points, taken from ancient Greece to Renaissance France, have parallels in such venues as the business and politics of modern society.

As I was working on this, the Egyptian people were having serious doubts about their president, Hosni Mubarak. Every day I would draw a page about how to handle similar situations, and every day Mubarak would do the opposite. Hosni Mubarak is no longer the president of Egypt.

People often criticize Machiavelli as being overly shrewd at best—or even cruel and cutthroat. I feel this is too succinct and dismissive of Machiavelli, his writing, and his intent. Most certainly cynical and sardonic, Machiavelli is a pragmatist first: committed to observation, human nature, history, and the facts. They may not be nice, they may not be pretty, but here they are; learn from them.

While Machiavelli's flair for language made adapting this comic a great gig, it also afforded me the opportunity to draw all kinds of fun stuff, which is really why you get into drawing in the first place. Knights, vikings, a Minotaur, the creation of Adam, Leonardo da Vinci. And pantaloons. Good God, I love drawing pantaloons. People often ask me what I like to draw, and never once have I thought to answer "pantaloons." These effete Renaissance-era roosters with their flippy hair and silly pomp proved to be some of the most fun I've ever had drawing.

You may or may not learn how to topple governments or navigate the intricacies of political discourse, but I hope you enjoy reading this book half as much as I enjoyed working on it.

Lastly, I'd like to thank a certain raven-haired beauty for her friendship and support while I worked on this. You certainly improved the view from my drawing board.

Pantaloons!

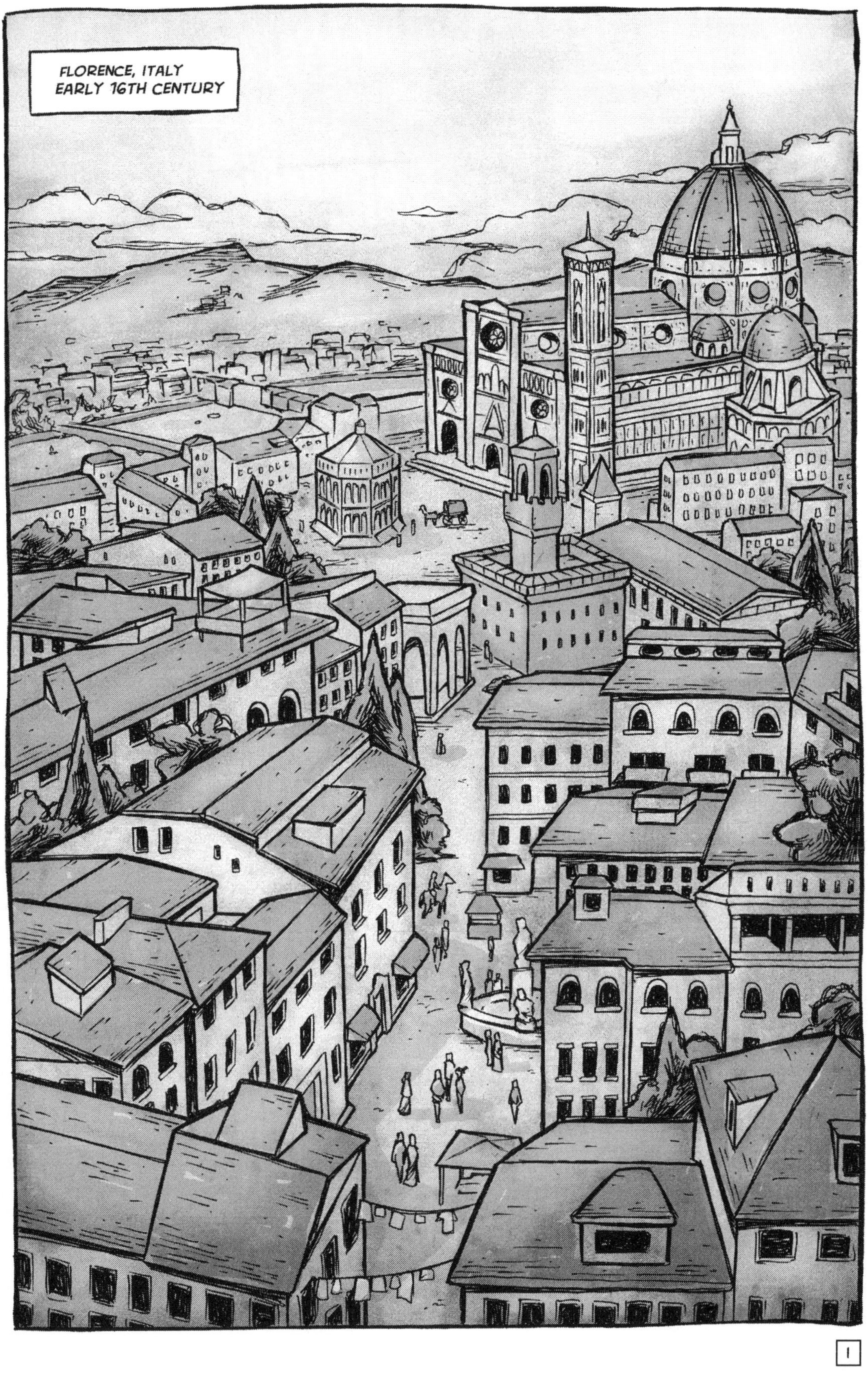
FLORENCE, ITALY
EARLY 16TH CENTURY

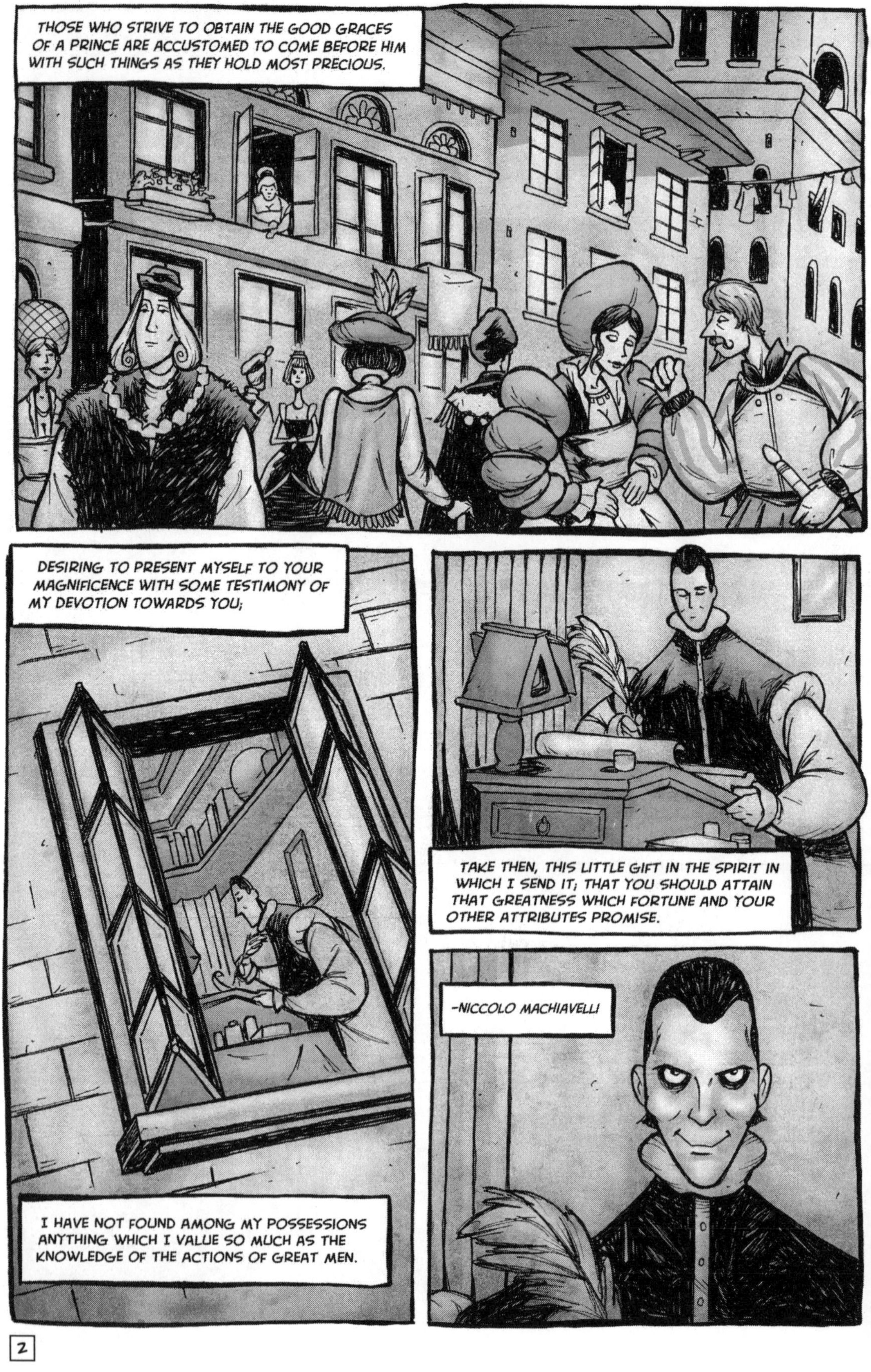
THOSE WHO STRIVE TO OBTAIN THE GOOD GRACES OF A PRINCE ARE ACCUSTOMED TO COME BEFORE HIM WITH SUCH THINGS AS THEY HOLD MOST PRECIOUS.
DESIRING TO PRESENT MYSELF TO YOUR MAGNIFICENCE WITH SOME TESTIMONY OF MY DEVOTION TOWARDS YOU;
I HAVE NOT FOUND AMONG MY POSSESSIONS ANYTHING WHICH I VALUE SO MUCH AS THE KNOWLEDGE OF THE ACTIONS OF GREAT MEN.
TAKE THEN, THIS LITTLE GIFT IN THE SPIRIT IN WHICH I SEND IT; THAT YOU SHOULD ATTAIN THAT GREATNESS WHICH FORTUNE AND YOUR OTHER ATTRIBUTES PROMISE.
-NICCOLO MACHIAVELLI

TYPES OF PRINCIPALITIES

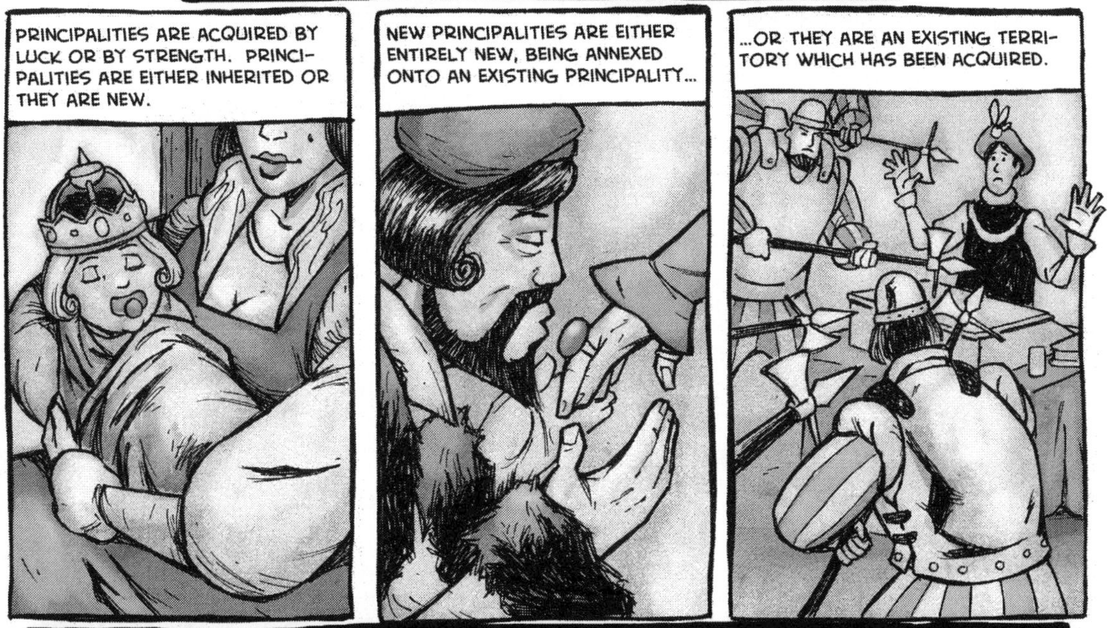
PRINCIPALITIES ARE ACQUIRED BY LUCK OR BY STRENGTH. PRINCIPALITIES ARE EITHER INHERITED OR THEY ARE NEW.
NEW PRINCIPALITIES ARE EITHER ENTIRELY NEW, BEING ANNEXED ONTO AN EXISTING PRINCIPALITY...
...OR THEY ARE AN EXISTING TERRITORY WHICH HAS BEEN ACQUIRED.

CONCERNING HEREDITARY PRINCIPALITIES

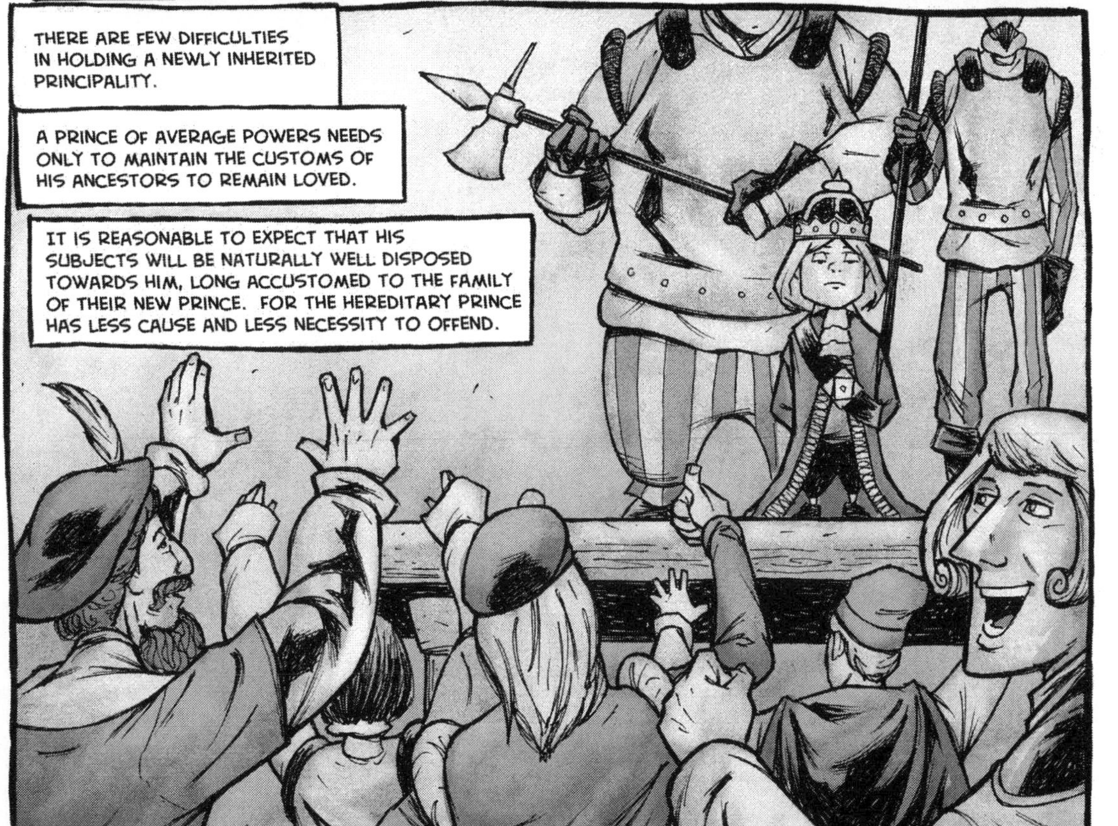
THERE ARE FEW DIFFICULTIES IN HOLDING A NEWLY INHERITED PRINCIPALITY.
A PRINCE OF AVERAGE POWERS NEEDS ONLY TO MAINTAIN THE CUSTOMS OF HIS ANCESTORS TO REMAIN LOVED.
IT IS REASONABLE TO EXPECT THAT HIS SUBJECTS WILL BE NATURALLY WELL DISPOSED TOWARDS HIM, LONG ACCUSTOMED TO THE FAMILY OF THEIR NEW PRINCE. FOR THE HEREDITARY PRINCE HAS LESS CAUSE AND LESS NECESSITY TO OFFEND.

CONCERNING MIXED PRINCIPALITIES

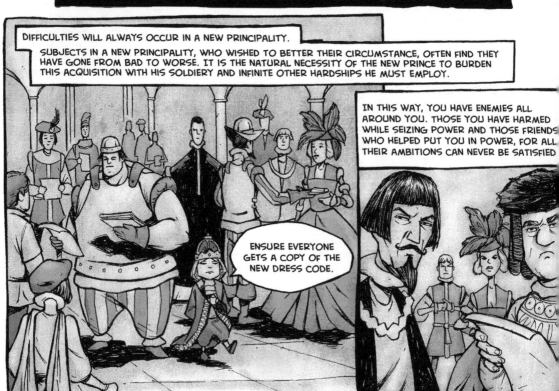

DIFFICULTIES WILL ALWAYS OCCUR IN A NEW PRINCIPALITY.

SUBJECTS IN A NEW PRINCIPALITY, WHO WISHED TO BETTER THEIR CIRCUMSTANCE, OFTEN FIND THEY HAVE GONE FROM BAD TO WORSE. IT IS THE NATURAL NECESSITY OF THE NEW PRINCE TO BURDEN THIS ACQUISITION WITH HIS SOLDIERY AND INFINITE OTHER HARDSHIPS HE MUST EMPLOY.

IN THIS WAY, YOU HAVE ENEMIES ALL AROUND YOU. THOSE YOU HAVE HARMED WHILE SEIZING POWER AND THOSE FRIENDS WHO HELPED PUT YOU IN POWER, FOR ALL THEIR AMBITIONS CAN NEVER BE SATISFIED

ENSURE EVERYONE GETS A COPY OF THE NEW DRESS CODE.

AN ANNEXED TERRITORY OF SIMILAR LOCATION AND CUSTOMS MAY BE EASILY KEPT, SO LONG AS THE FORMER LORD AND FAMILY IS EXTINGUISHED; AND THAT THEIR CUSTOMS AND LIFESTYLE REMAIN SIMILAR.

IN A VERY SHORT TIME THEY WILL BECOME ONE BODY WITH THE OLD PRINCIPALITY.

BUT IF NEW ACQUISITIONS ARE DIFFERENT IN LANGUAGE AND CUSTOMS, THEY ARE DIFFICULT TO KEEP. IT IS BEST TO LIVE THERE YOURSELF, TO PROTECT AGAINST OUTSIDE POWERS AND TO WEAKEN STRONG FACTIONS WITHIN THE PRINCIPALITY.

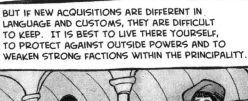

IF THAT IS NOT POSSIBLE, ONE MUST BE CAREFUL TO NOT GRANT ONE'S REPRESENTATIVES TOO MUCH POWER, FOR TO MAKE OTHERS POWERFUL IS TO WEAKEN ONESELF.

RESIDING IN AN ACQUIRED TERRITORY MAKES THE POSITION MORE SECURE AND DURABLE, AS IT HAS MADE THAT OF THE TURK IN GREECE.

IF HE HAD NOT SETTLED THERE, HE WOULD NOT HAVE BEEN ABLE TO KEEP IT.

BECAUSE IF ONE IS ON THE SPOT, DISORDERS ARE SEEN AS THEY SPRING UP, AND ONE CAN QUICKLY REMEDY THEM.

BUT IF ONE IS NOT AT HAND, THEY ARE HEARD OF ONLY WHEN THEY ARE GREAT, AND THEN ONE CAN NO LONGER REMEDY THEM.

TURKS GO HOME

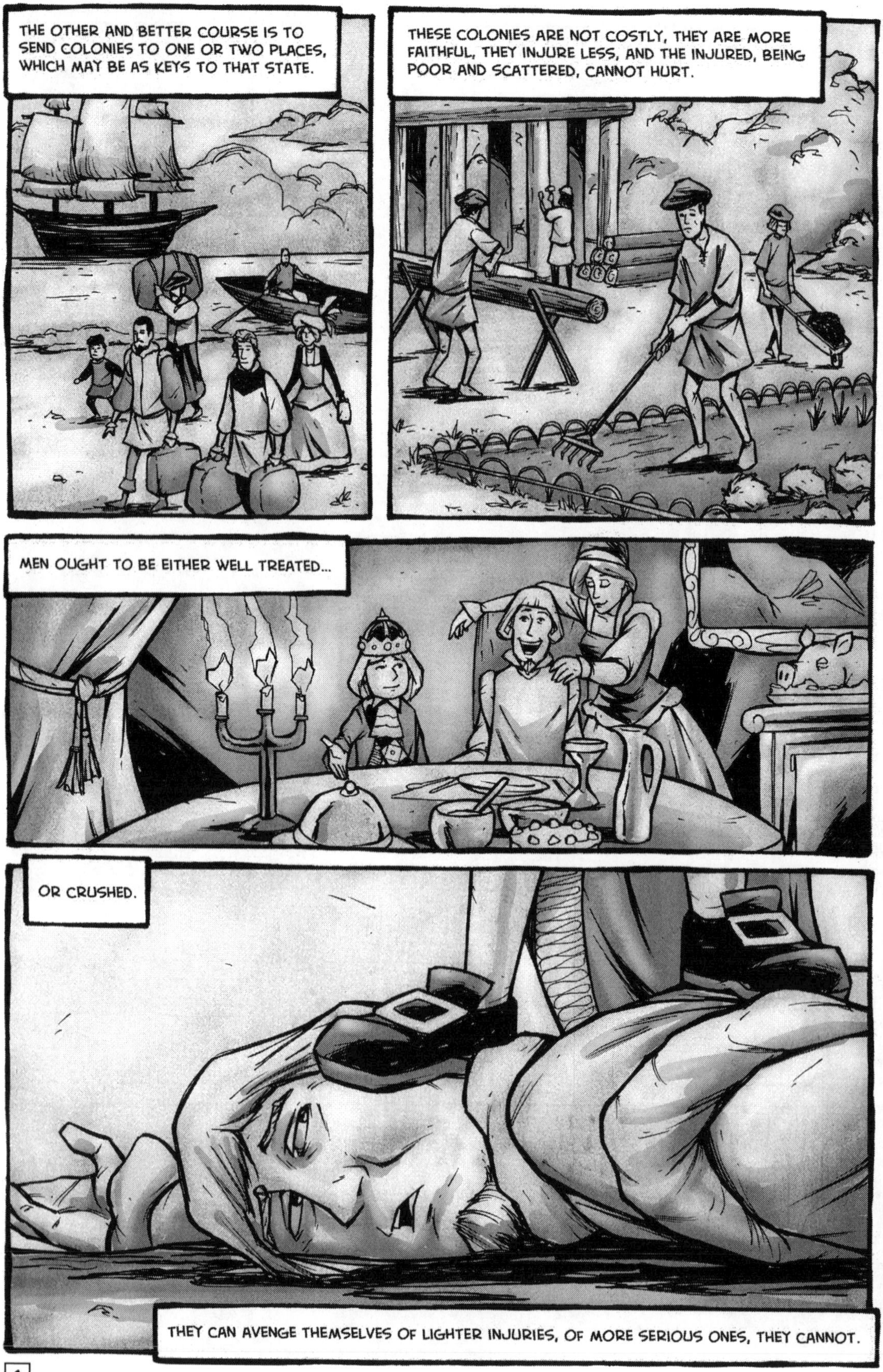
THE OTHER AND BETTER COURSE IS TO SEND COLONIES TO ONE OR TWO PLACES, WHICH MAY BE AS KEYS TO THAT STATE.
THESE COLONIES ARE NOT COSTLY, THEY ARE MORE FAITHFUL, THEY INJURE LESS, AND THE INJURED, BEING POOR AND SCATTERED, CANNOT HURT.
MEN OUGHT TO BE EITHER WELL TREATED...
OR CRUSHED.
THEY CAN AVENGE THEMSELVES OF LIGHTER INJURIES, OF MORE SERIOUS ONES, THEY CANNOT.

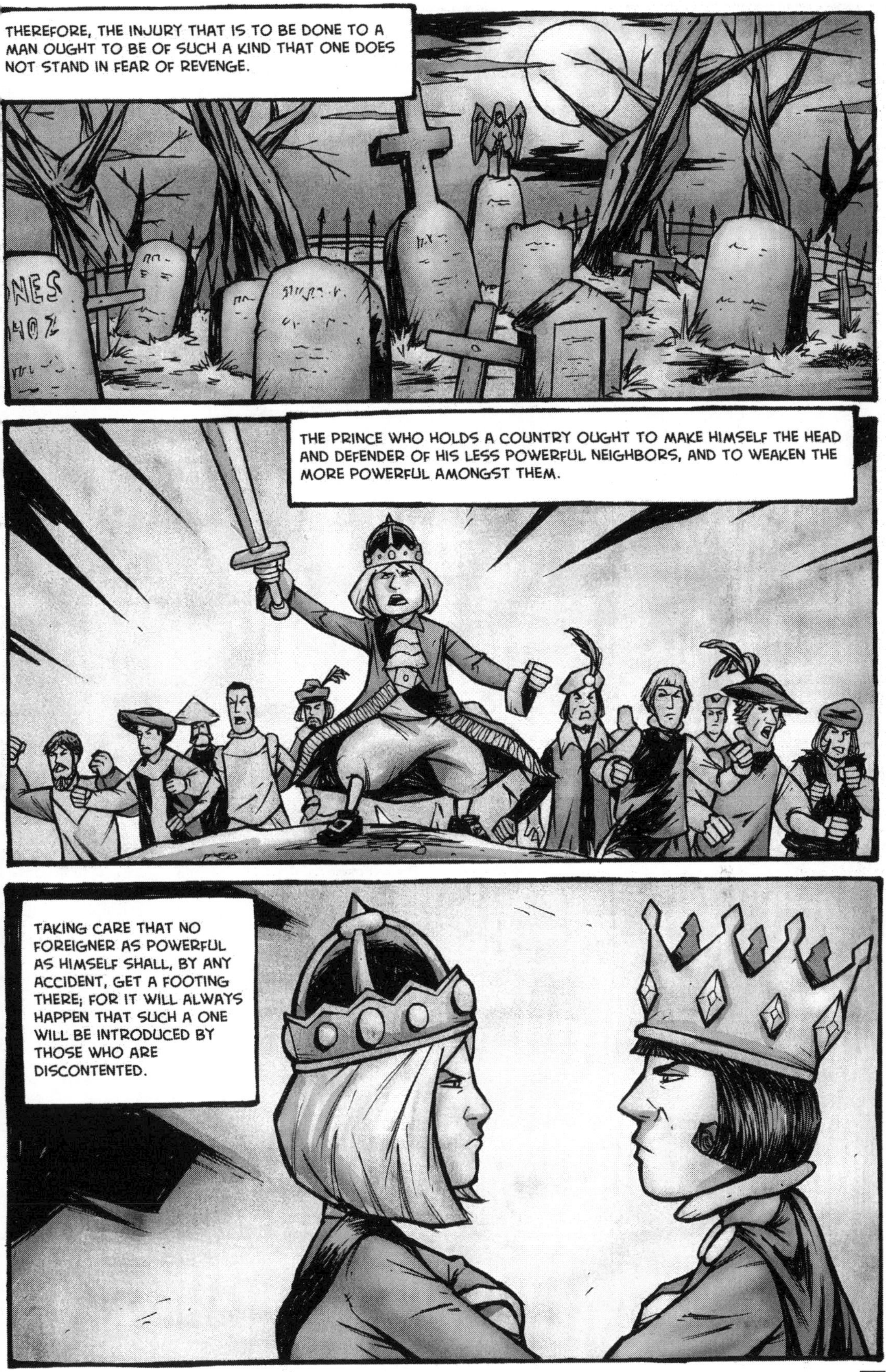
THEREFORE, THE INJURY THAT IS TO BE DONE TO A MAN OUGHT TO BE OF SUCH A KIND THAT ONE DOES NOT STAND IN FEAR OF REVENGE.
THE PRINCE WHO HOLDS A COUNTRY OUGHT TO MAKE HIMSELF THE HEAD AND DEFENDER OF HIS LESS POWERFUL NEIGHBORS, AND TO WEAKEN THE MORE POWERFUL AMONGST THEM.
TAKING CARE THAT NO FOREIGNER AS POWERFUL AS HIMSELF SHALL, BY ANY ACCIDENT, GET A FOOTING THERE; FOR IT WILL ALWAYS HAPPEN THAT SUCH A ONE WILL BE INTRODUCED BY THOSE WHO ARE DISCONTENTED.

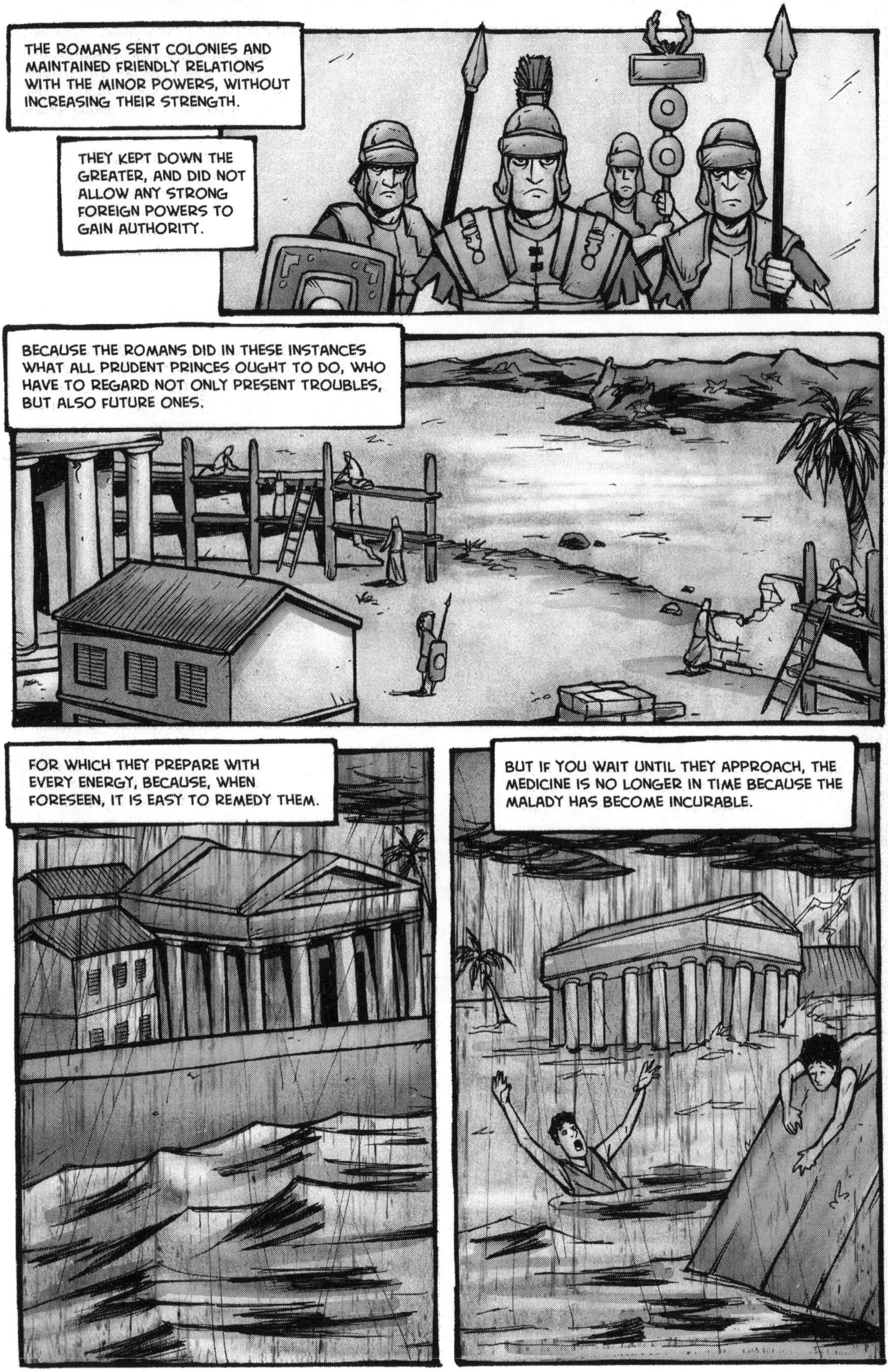
THE ROMANS SENT COLONIES AND MAINTAINED FRIENDLY RELATIONS WITH THE MINOR POWERS, WITHOUT INCREASING THEIR STRENGTH.
THEY KEPT DOWN THE GREATER, AND DID NOT ALLOW ANY STRONG FOREIGN POWERS TO GAIN AUTHORITY.
BECAUSE THE ROMANS DID IN THESE INSTANCES WHAT ALL PRUDENT PRINCES OUGHT TO DO, WHO HAVE TO REGARD NOT ONLY PRESENT TROUBLES, BUT ALSO FUTURE ONES.
FOR WHICH THEY PREPARE WITH EVERY ENERGY, BECAUSE, WHEN FORESEEN, IT IS EASY TO REMEDY THEM.
BUT IF YOU WAIT UNTIL THEY APPROACH, THE MEDICINE IS NO LONGER IN TIME BECAUSE THE MALADY HAS BECOME INCURABLE.

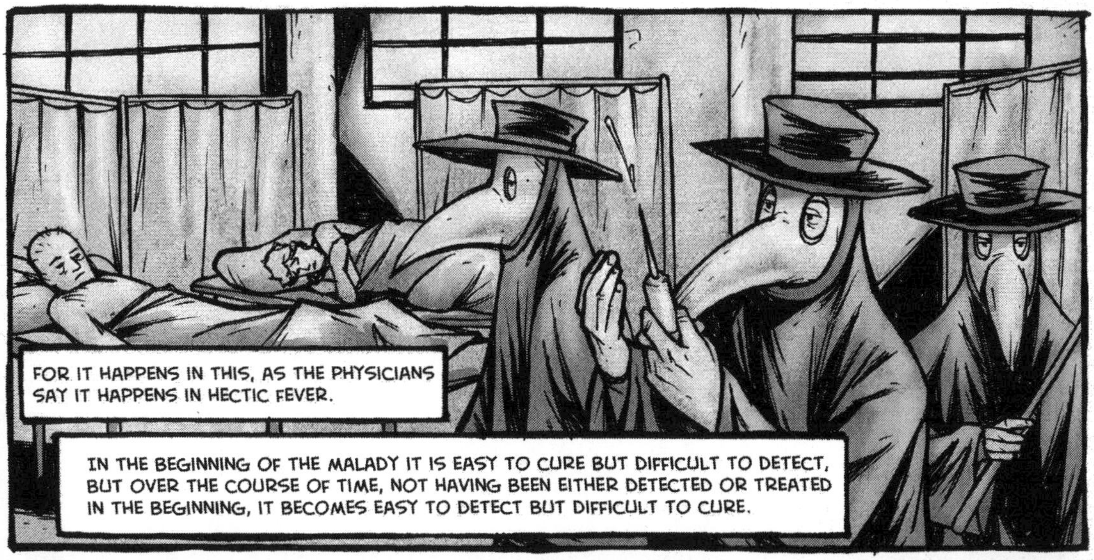
FOR IT HAPPENS IN THIS, AS THE PHYSICIANS SAY IT HAPPENS IN HECTIC FEVER.
IN THE BEGINNING OF THE MALADY IT IS EASY TO CURE BUT DIFFICULT TO DETECT, BUT OVER THE COURSE OF TIME, NOT HAVING BEEN EITHER DETECTED OR TREATED IN THE BEGINNING, IT BECOMES EASY TO DETECT BUT DIFFICULT TO CURE.

WHY THE KINGDOM OF DARIUS, CONQUERED BY ALEXANDER, DID NOT REBEL AGAINST THE SUCCESSORS OF ALEXANDER AT HIS DEATH

PRINCIPALITIES ARE FOUND TO BE GOVERNED IN TWO DIFFERENT WAYS; EITHER BY A PRINCE, WITH A BODY OF SERVANTS, WHO ASSIST HIM TO GOVERN THE KINGDOM BY HIS FAVOR AND PERMISSION...

...OR BY A PRINCE AND BARONS, WHO HOLD THAT DIGNITY BY ANTIQUITY OF BLOOD AND NOT BY THE GRACE OF THE KING.

EXAMPLES OF THESE ARE THE TURKISH SULTAN AND THE KING OF FRANCE.

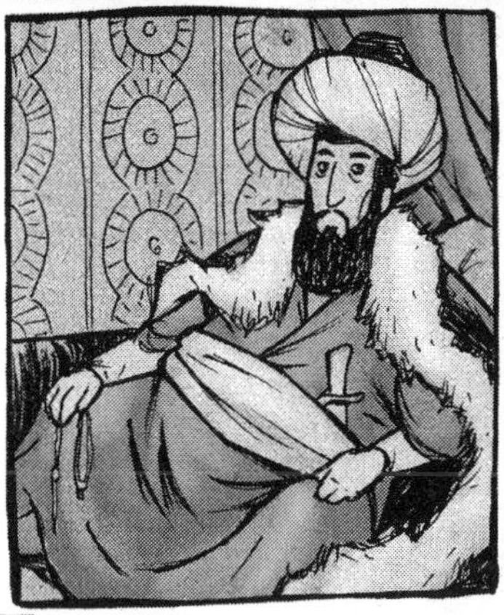

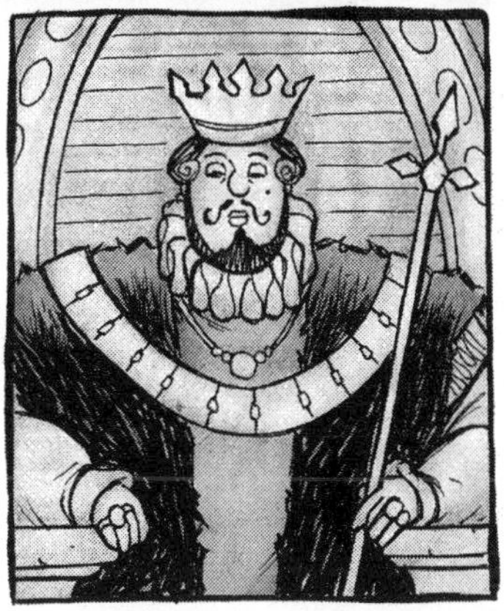

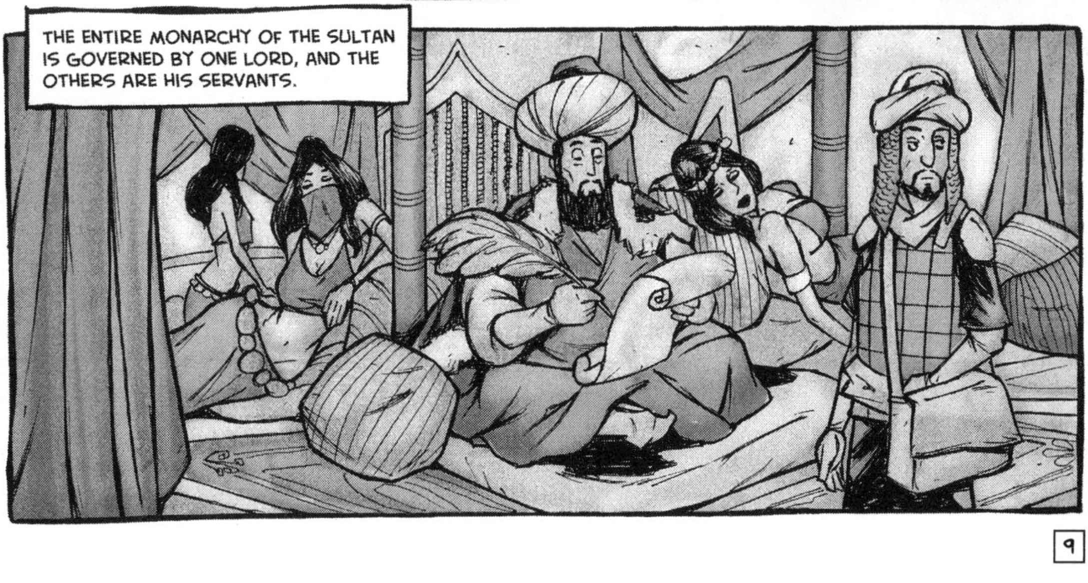
THE ENTIRE MONARCHY OF THE SULTAN IS GOVERNED BY ONE LORD, AND THE OTHERS ARE HIS SERVANTS.

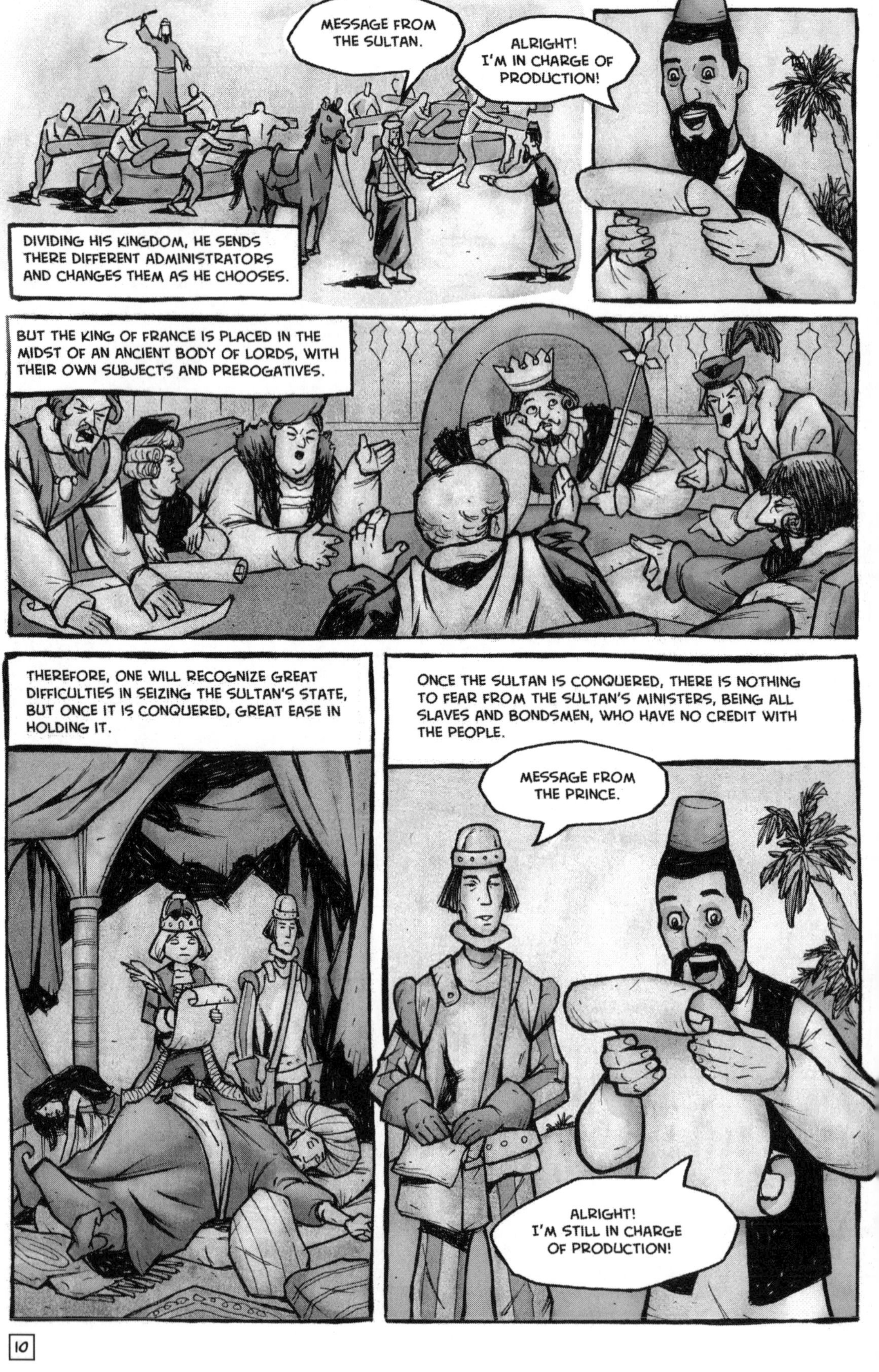
DIVIDING HIS KINGDOM, HE SENDS THERE DIFFERENT ADMINISTRATORS AND CHANGES THEM AS HE CHOOSES.
MESSAGE FROM THE SULTAN.
ALRIGHT! I'M IN CHARGE OF PRODUCTION!
BUT THE KING OF FRANCE IS PLACED IN THE MIDST OF AN ANCIENT BODY OF LORDS, WITH THEIR OWN SUBJECTS AND PREROGATIVES.
THEREFORE, ONE WILL RECOGNIZE GREAT DIFFICULTIES IN SEIZING THE SULTAN'S STATE, BUT ONCE IT IS CONQUERED, GREAT EASE IN HOLDING IT.
ONCE THE SULTAN IS CONQUERED, THERE IS NOTHING TO FEAR FROM THE SULTAN'S MINISTERS, BEING ALL SLAVES AND BONDSMEN, WHO HAVE NO CREDIT WITH THE PEOPLE.
MESSAGE FROM THE PRINCE.
ALRIGHT! I'M STILL IN CHARGE OF PRODUCTION!

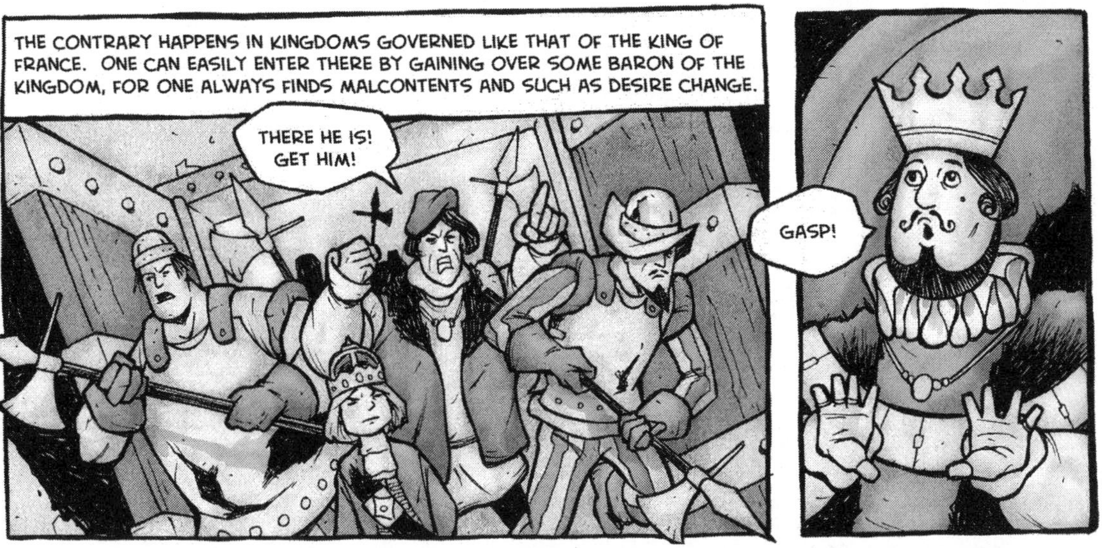
THE CONTRARY HAPPENS IN KINGDOMS GOVERNED LIKE THAT OF THE KING OF FRANCE. ONE CAN EASILY ENTER THERE BY GAINING OVER SOME BARON OF THE KINGDOM, FOR ONE ALWAYS FINDS MALCONTENTS AND SUCH AS DESIRE CHANGE.
THERE HE IS! GET HIM!
GASP!

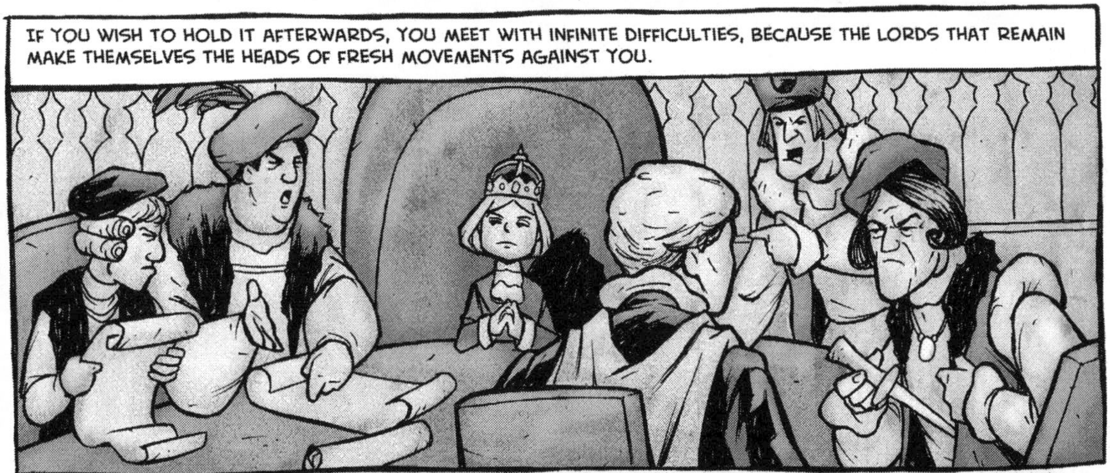
IF YOU WISH TO HOLD IT AFTERWARDS, YOU MEET WITH INFINITE DIFFICULTIES, BECAUSE THE LORDS THAT REMAIN MAKE THEMSELVES THE HEADS OF FRESH MOVEMENTS AGAINST YOU.

CONCERNING NEW PRINCIPALITIES WHICH ARE ACQUIRED BY ONE'S OWN ARMS AND ABILITY

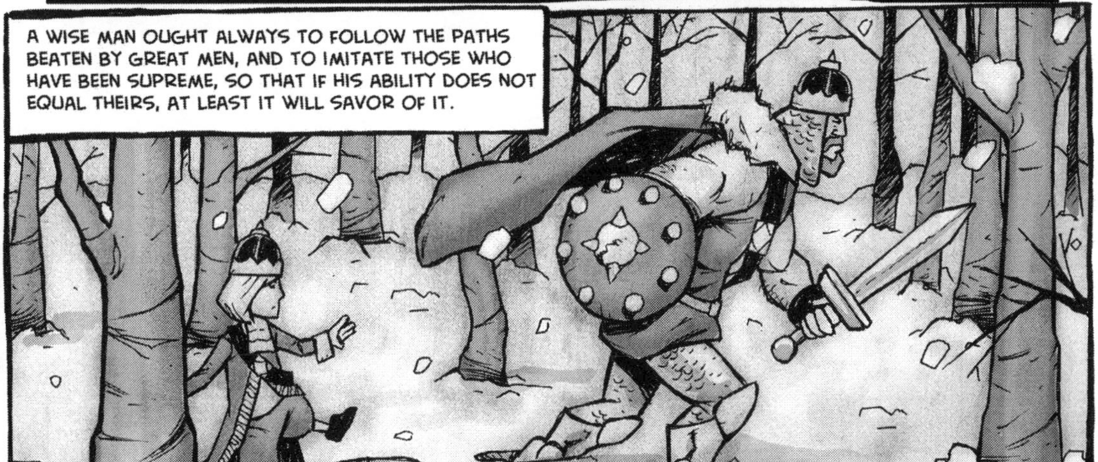
A WISE MAN OUGHT ALWAYS TO FOLLOW THE PATHS BEATEN BY GREAT MEN, AND TO IMITATE THOSE WHO HAVE BEEN SUPREME, SO THAT IF HIS ABILITY DOES NOT EQUAL THEIRS, AT LEAST IT WILL SAVOR OF IT.

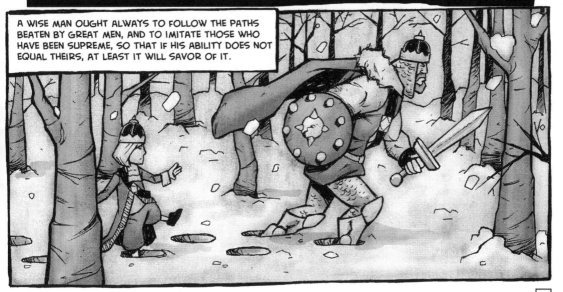

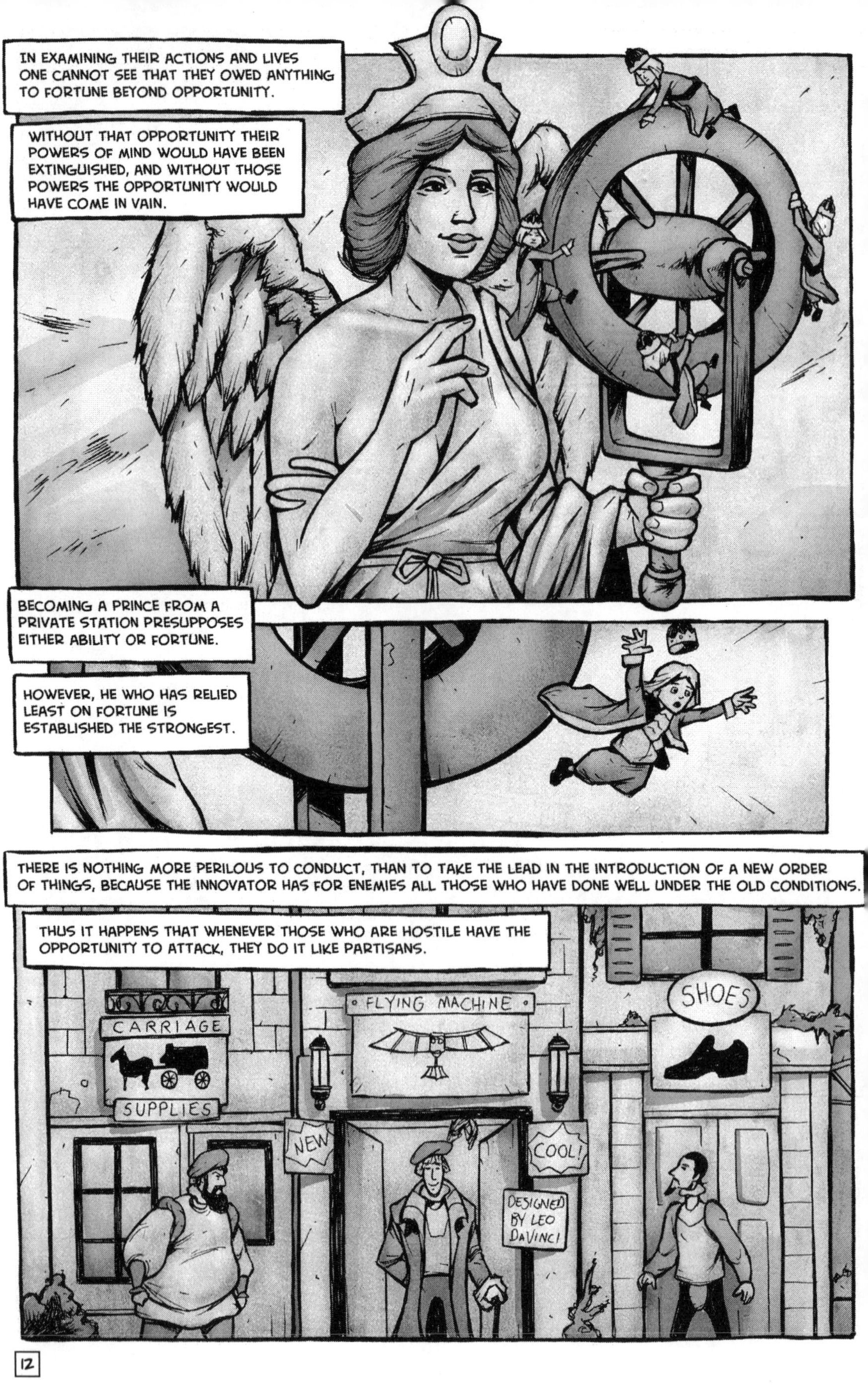

IN EXAMINING THEIR ACTIONS AND LIVES ONE CANNOT SEE THAT THEY OWED ANYTHING TO FORTUNE BEYOND OPPORTUNITY.
WITHOUT THAT OPPORTUNITY THEIR POWERS OF MIND WOULD HAVE BEEN EXTINGUISHED, AND WITHOUT THOSE POWERS THE OPPORTUNITY WOULD HAVE COME IN VAIN.
BECOMING A PRINCE FROM A PRIVATE STATION PRESUPPOSES EITHER ABILITY OR FORTUNE.
HOWEVER, HE WHO HAS RELIED LEAST ON FORTUNE IS ESTABLISHED THE STRONGEST.
THERE IS NOTHING MORE PERILOUS TO CONDUCT, THAN TO TAKE THE LEAD IN THE INTRODUCTION OF A NEW ORDER OF THINGS, BECAUSE THE INNOVATOR HAS FOR ENEMIES ALL THOSE WHO HAVE DONE WELL UNDER THE OLD CONDITIONS.
THUS IT HAPPENS THAT WHENEVER THOSE WHO ARE HOSTILE HAVE THE OPPORTUNITY TO ATTACK, THEY DO IT LIKE PARTISANS.
CARRIAGE
SUPPLIES
FLYING MACHINE
SHOES
NEW
COOL!
DESIGNED BY LEO DAVINCI

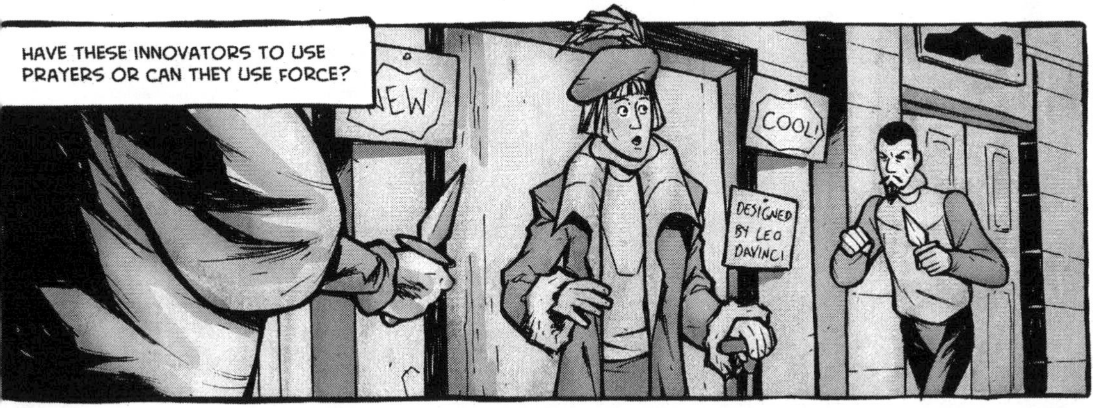
HAVE THESE INNOVATORS TO USE PRAYERS OR CAN THEY USE FORCE?
NEW
COOL!
DESIGNED BY LEO DAVINCI

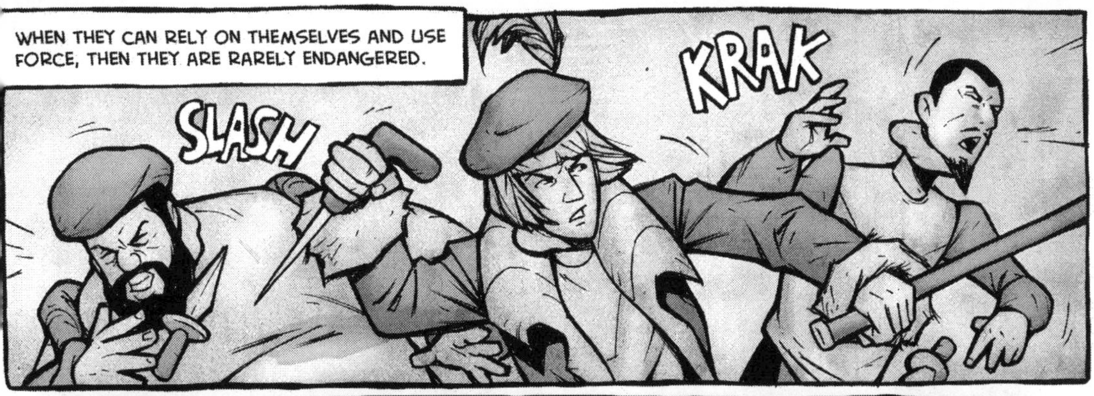
WHEN THEY CAN RELY ON THEMSELVES AND USE FORCE, THEN THEY ARE RARELY ENDANGERED.
SLASH
KRAK

CONCERNING NEW PRINCIPALITIES WHICH ARE ACQUIRED EITHER BY THE ARMS OF OTHERS OR BY GOOD FORTUNE

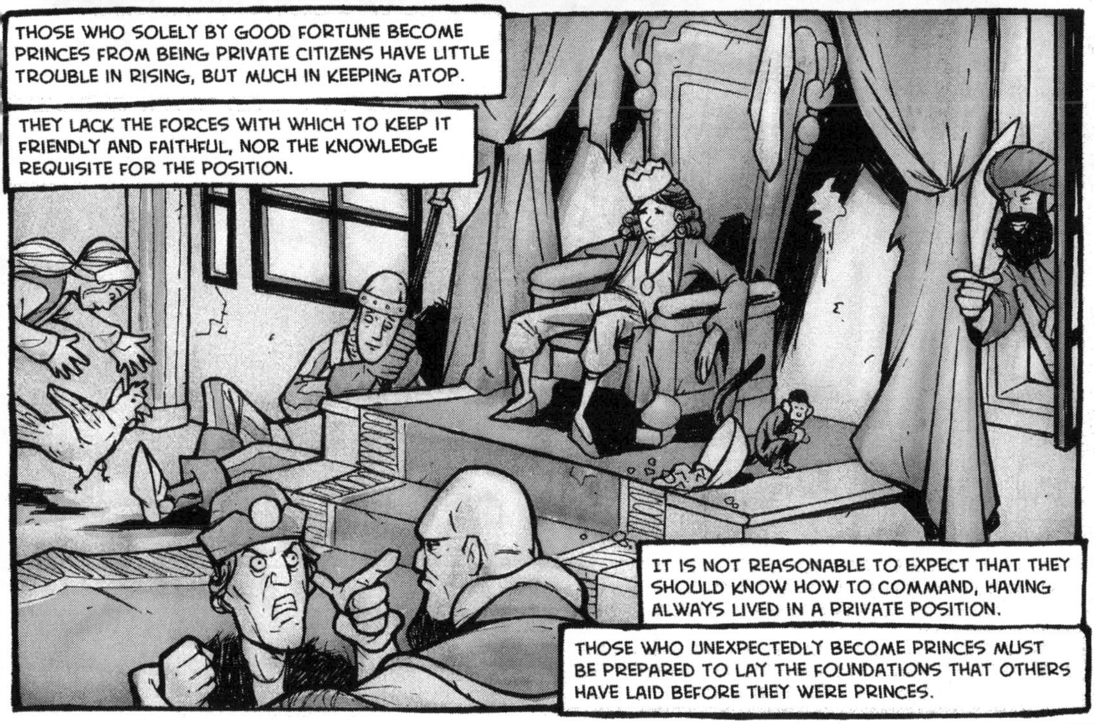
THOSE WHO SOLELY BY GOOD FORTUNE BECOME PRINCES FROM BEING PRIVATE CITIZENS HAVE LITTLE TROUBLE IN RISING, BUT MUCH IN KEEPING ATOP.
THEY LACK THE FORCES WITH WHICH TO KEEP IT FRIENDLY AND FAITHFUL, NOR THE KNOWLEDGE REQUISITE FOR THE POSITION.
IT IS NOT REASONABLE TO EXPECT THAT THEY SHOULD KNOW HOW TO COMMAND, HAVING ALWAYS LIVED IN A PRIVATE POSITION.
THOSE WHO UNEXPECTEDLY BECOME PRINCES MUST BE PREPARED TO LAY THE FOUNDATIONS THAT OTHERS HAVE LAID BEFORE THEY WERE PRINCES.

CONCERNING THOSE WHO HAVE OBTAINED A PRINCIPALITY BY WICKEDNESS.

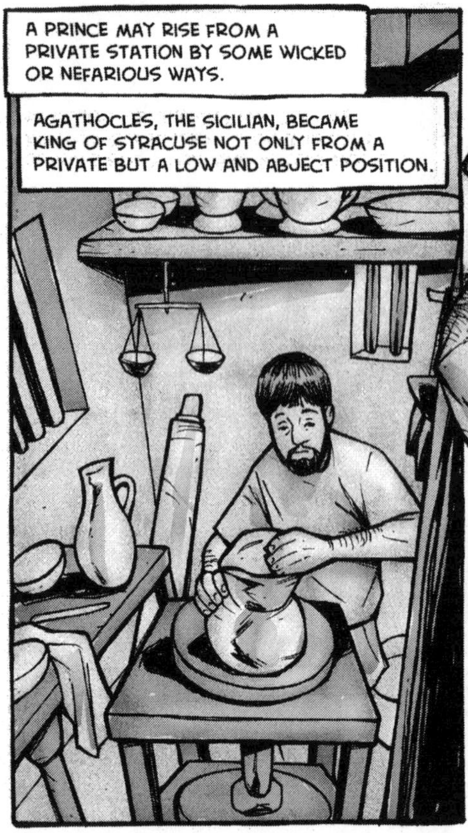
A PRINCE MAY RISE FROM A PRIVATE STATION BY SOME WICKED OR NEFARIOUS WAYS.
AGATHOCLES, THE SICILIAN, BECAME KING OF SYRACUSE NOT ONLY FROM A PRIVATE BUT A LOW AND ABJECT POSITION.

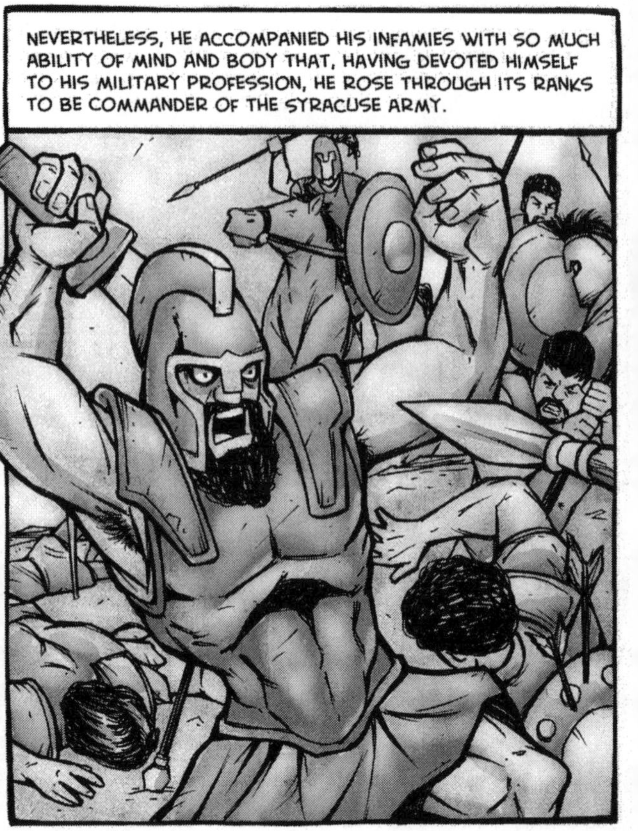
NEVERTHELESS, HE ACCOMPANIED HIS INFAMIES WITH SO MUCH ABILITY OF MIND AND BODY THAT, HAVING DEVOTED HIMSELF TO HIS MILITARY PROFESSION, HE ROSE THROUGH ITS RANKS TO BE COMMANDER OF THE SYRACUSE ARMY.

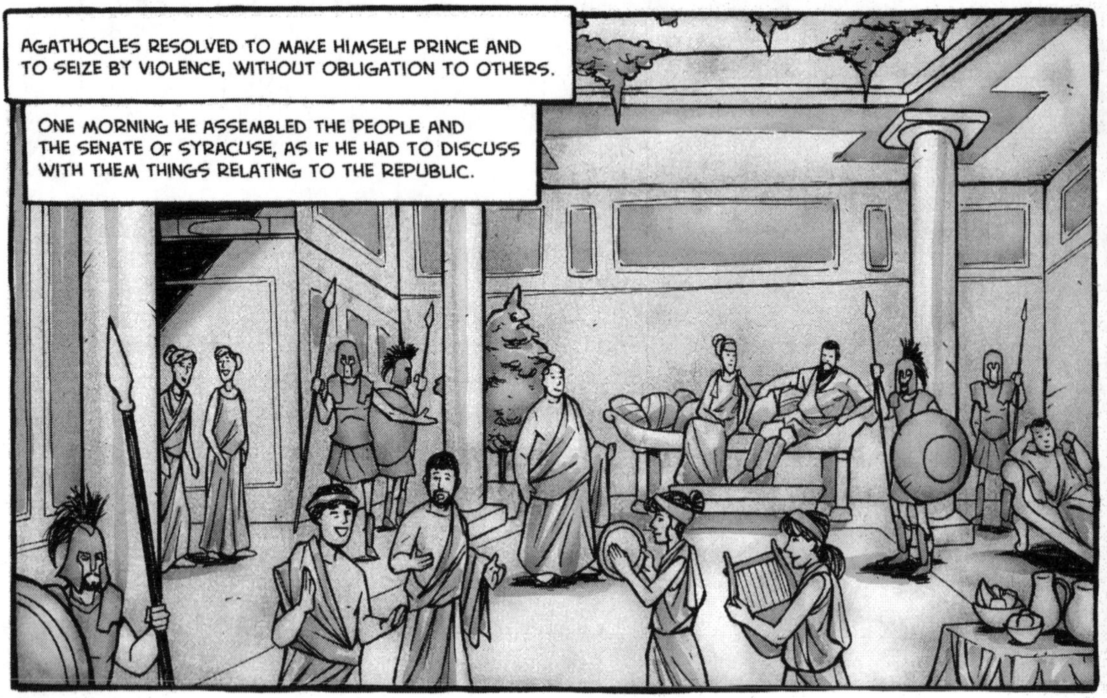
AGATHOCLES RESOLVED TO MAKE HIMSELF PRINCE AND TO SEIZE BY VIOLENCE, WITHOUT OBLIGATION TO OTHERS.
ONE MORNING HE ASSEMBLED THE PEOPLE AND THE SENATE OF SYRACUSE, AS IF HE HAD TO DISCUSS WITH THEM THINGS RELATING TO THE REPUBLIC.

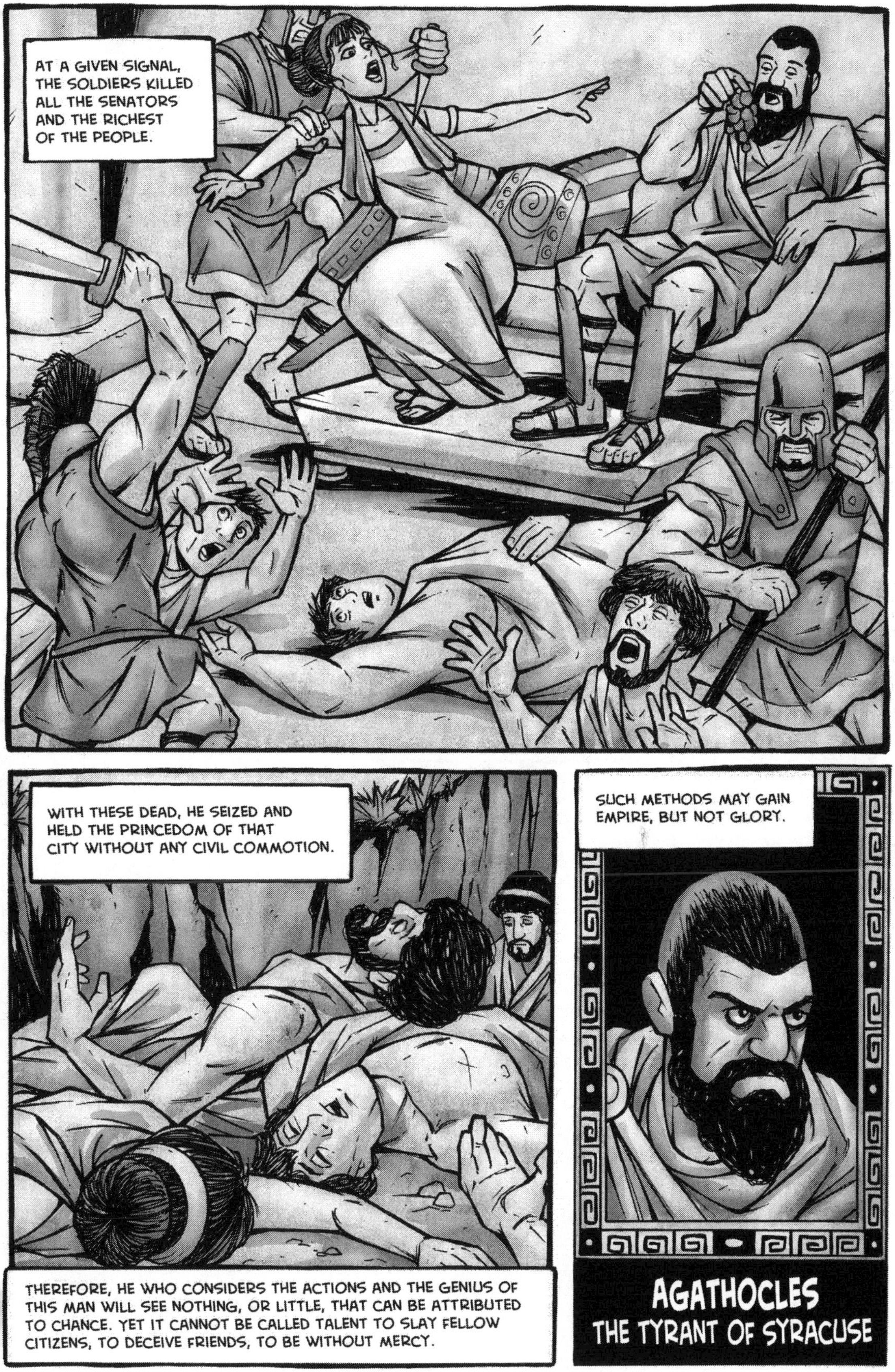
AT A GIVEN SIGNAL, THE SOLDIERS KILLED ALL THE SENATORS AND THE RICHEST OF THE PEOPLE.
WITH THESE DEAD, HE SEIZED AND HELD THE PRINCEDOM OF THAT CITY WITHOUT ANY CIVIL COMMOTION.
THEREFORE, HE WHO CONSIDERS THE ACTIONS AND THE GENIUS OF THIS MAN WILL SEE NOTHING, OR LITTLE, THAT CAN BE ATTRIBUTED TO CHANCE. YET IT CANNOT BE CALLED TALENT TO SLAY FELLOW CITIZENS, TO DECEIVE FRIENDS, TO BE WITHOUT MERCY.
SUCH METHODS MAY GAIN EMPIRE, BUT NOT GLORY.
AGATHOCLES
THE TYRANT OF SYRACUSE

CONCERNING A CIVIL PRINCIPALITY

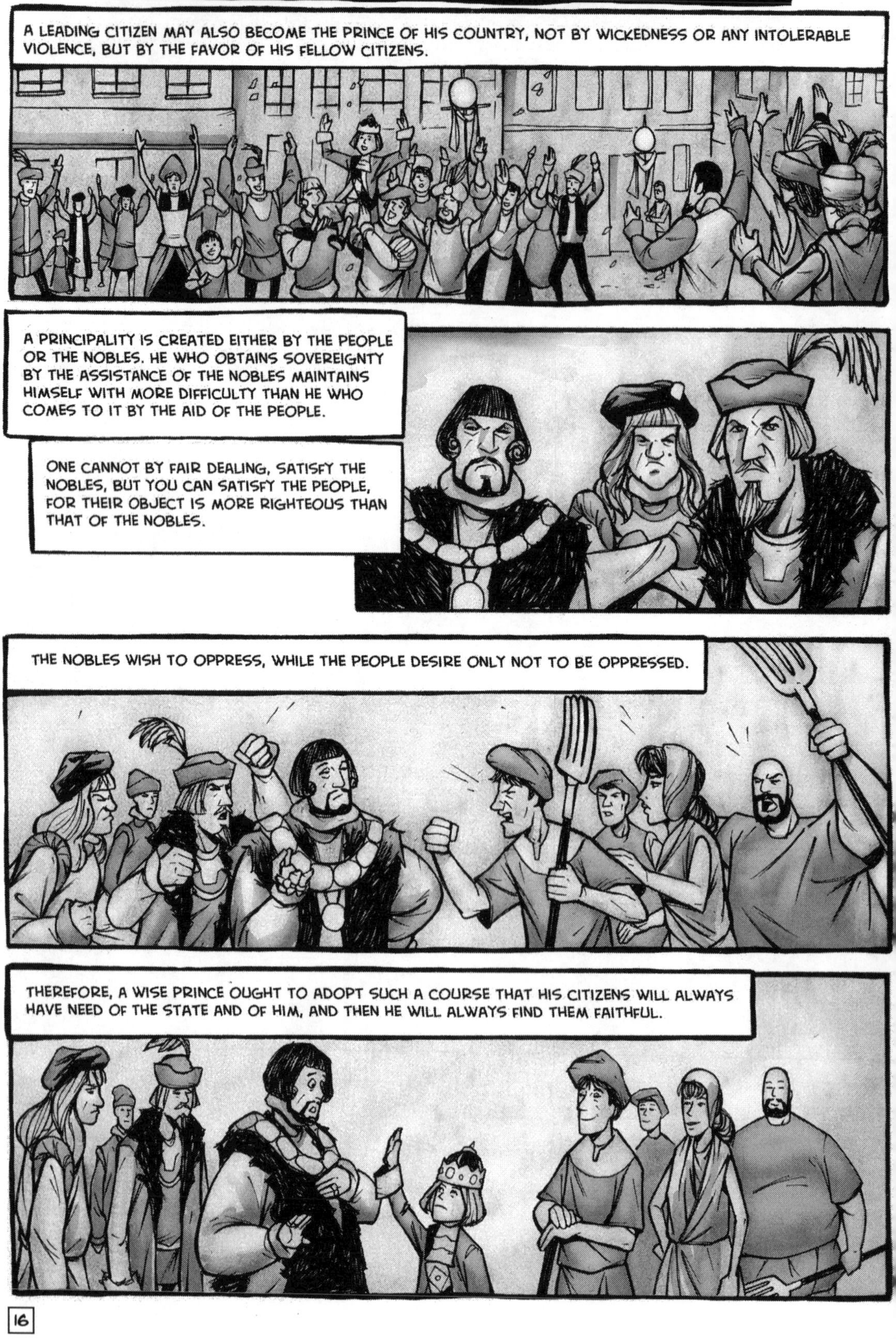

A LEADING CITIZEN MAY ALSO BECOME THE PRINCE OF HIS COUNTRY, NOT BY WICKEDNESS OR ANY INTOLERABLE VIOLENCE, BUT BY THE FAVOR OF HIS FELLOW CITIZENS.
A PRINCIPALITY IS CREATED EITHER BY THE PEOPLE OR THE NOBLES. HE WHO OBTAINS SOVEREIGNTY BY THE ASSISTANCE OF THE NOBLES MAINTAINS HIMSELF WITH MORE DIFFICULTY THAN HE WHO COMES TO IT BY THE AID OF THE PEOPLE.
ONE CANNOT BY FAIR DEALING, SATISFY THE NOBLES, BUT YOU CAN SATISFY THE PEOPLE, FOR THEIR OBJECT IS MORE RIGHTEOUS THAN THAT OF THE NOBLES.
THE NOBLES WISH TO OPPRESS, WHILE THE PEOPLE DESIRE ONLY NOT TO BE OPPRESSED.
THEREFORE, A WISE PRINCE OUGHT TO ADOPT SUCH A COURSE THAT HIS CITIZENS WILL ALWAYS HAVE NEED OF THE STATE AND OF HIM, AND THEN HE WILL ALWAYS FIND THEM FAITHFUL.

CONCERNING THE WAY IN WHICH THE STRENGTH OF ALL PRINCIPALITIES OUGHT TO BE MEASURED

IT IS NECESSARY TO CONSIDER WHETHER A PRINCE HAS SUCH POWER THAT HE CAN SUPPORT HIMSELF WITH HIS OWN RESOURCES, OR WHETHER HE HAS ALWAYS NEED OF THE ASSISTANCE OF OTHERS.

THOSE WHO ARE ABLE TO SUPPORT THEMSELVES ARE THOSE WHO CAN RAISE A SUFFICIENT ARMY TO JOIN BATTLE AGAINST ANYONE WHO COMES TO ATTACK THEM.

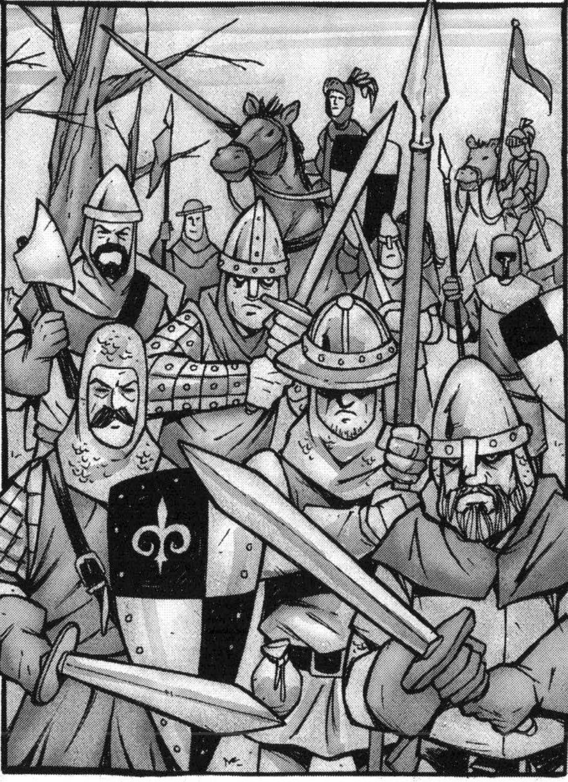

THOSE WHO HAVE NEED OF OTHERS CANNOT SHOW THEMSELVES AGAINST THE ENEMY IN THE FIELD, BUT ARE FORCED TO DEFEND THEMSELVES BY SHELTERING BEHIND WALLS.

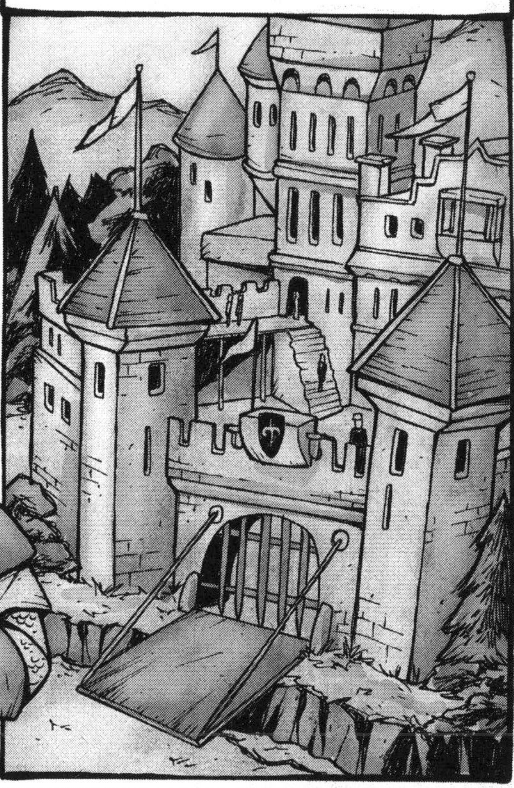

IF EVERYTHING IS WELL CONSIDERED, IT WILL NOT BE DIFFICULT FOR A WISE PRINCE TO KEEP THE MINDS OF HIS CITIZENS STEADFAST FROM FIRST TO LAST, WHEN HE DOES NOT FAIL TO SUPPORT AND DEFEND THEM.

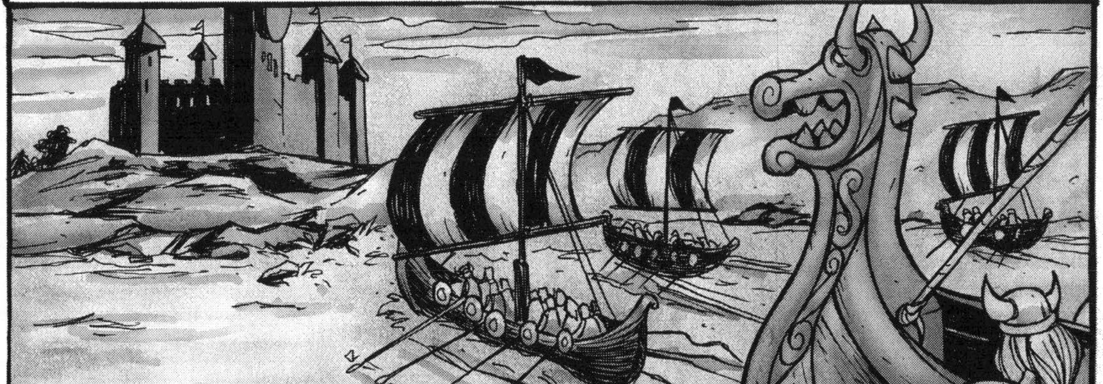

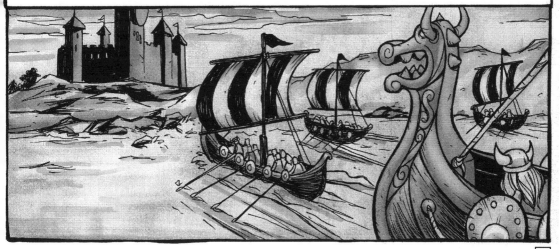

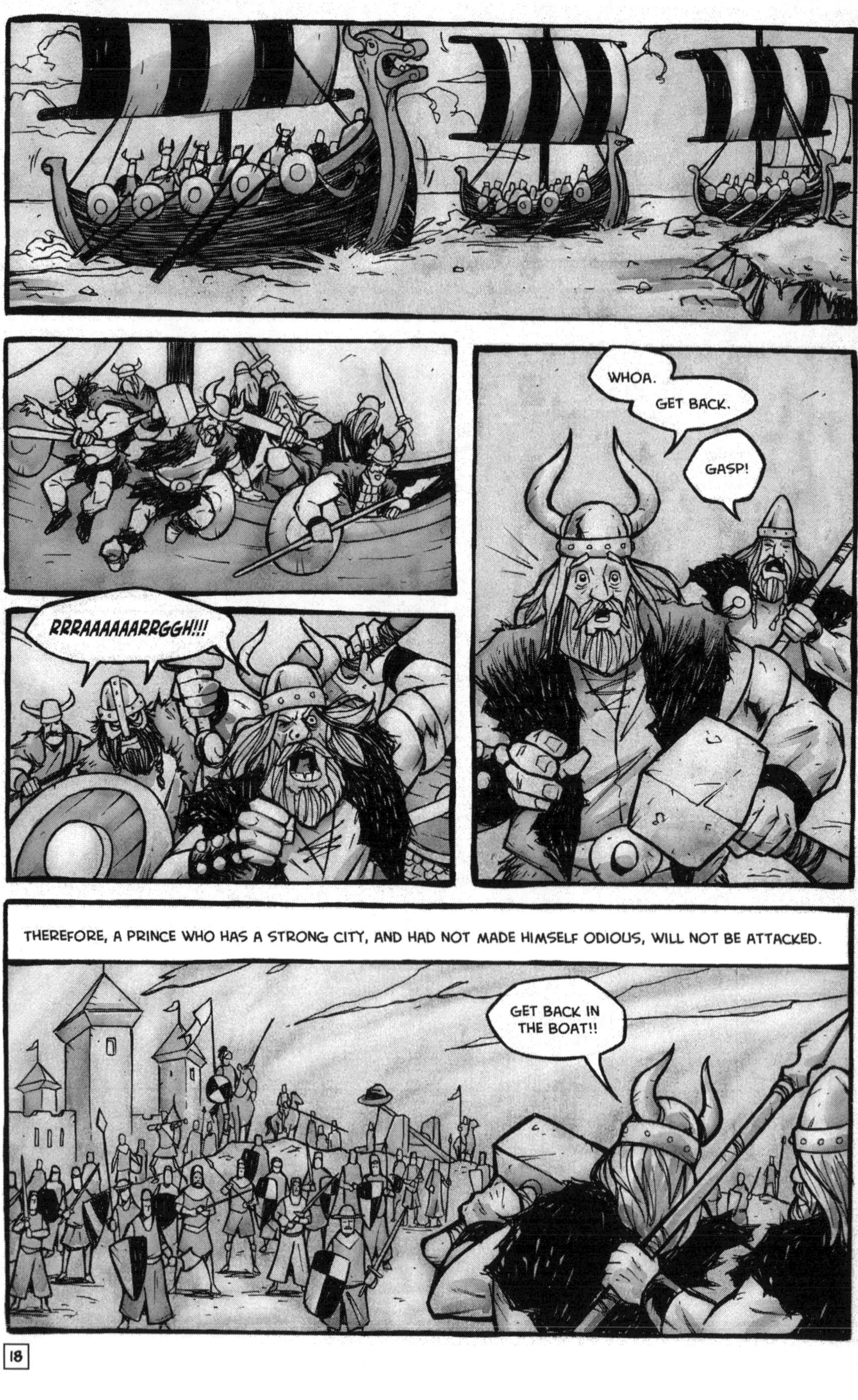
WHOA.
GET BACK.
GASP!
RRRAAAAAAARRGGH!!!
THEREFORE, A PRINCE WHO HAS A STRONG CITY, AND HAD NOT MADE HIMSELF ODIOUS, WILL NOT BE ATTACKED.
GET BACK IN THE BOAT!!

CONCERNING ECCLESIASTICAL PRINCIPALITIES

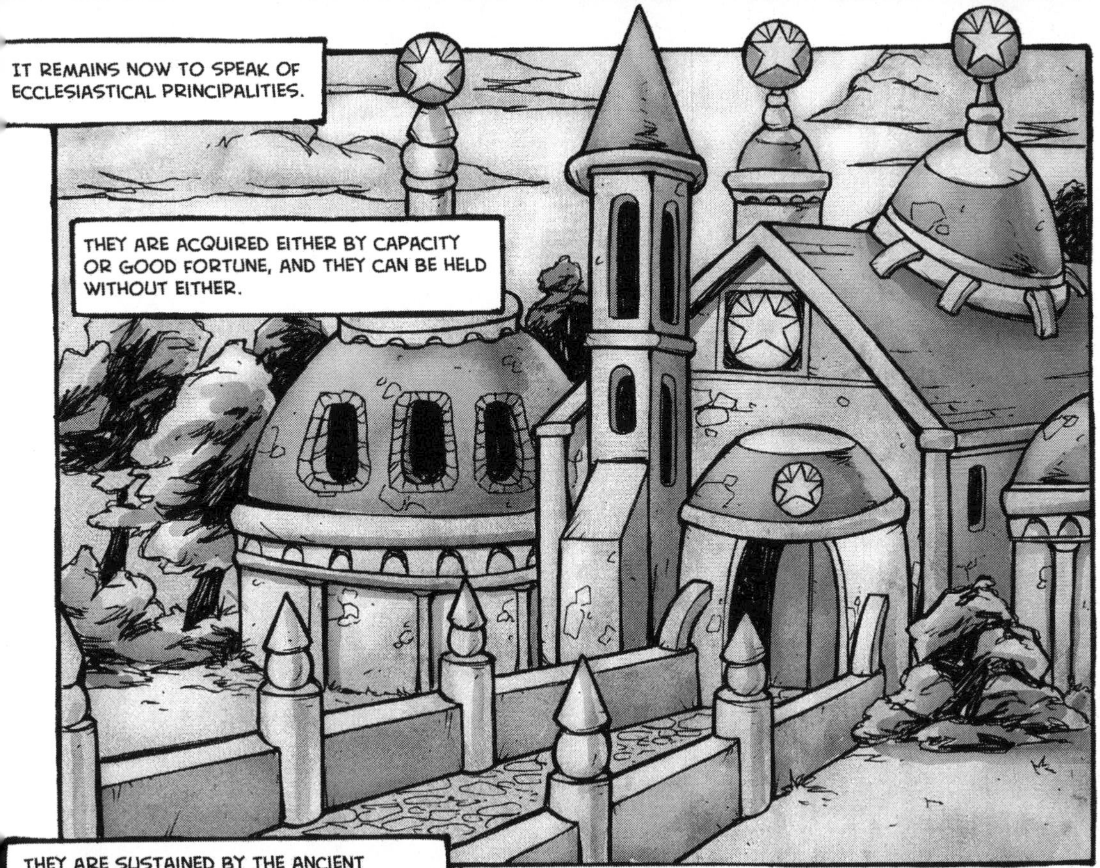
IT REMAINS NOW TO SPEAK OF ECCLESIASTICAL PRINCIPALITIES.
THEY ARE ACQUIRED EITHER BY CAPACITY OR GOOD FORTUNE, AND THEY CAN BE HELD WITHOUT EITHER.

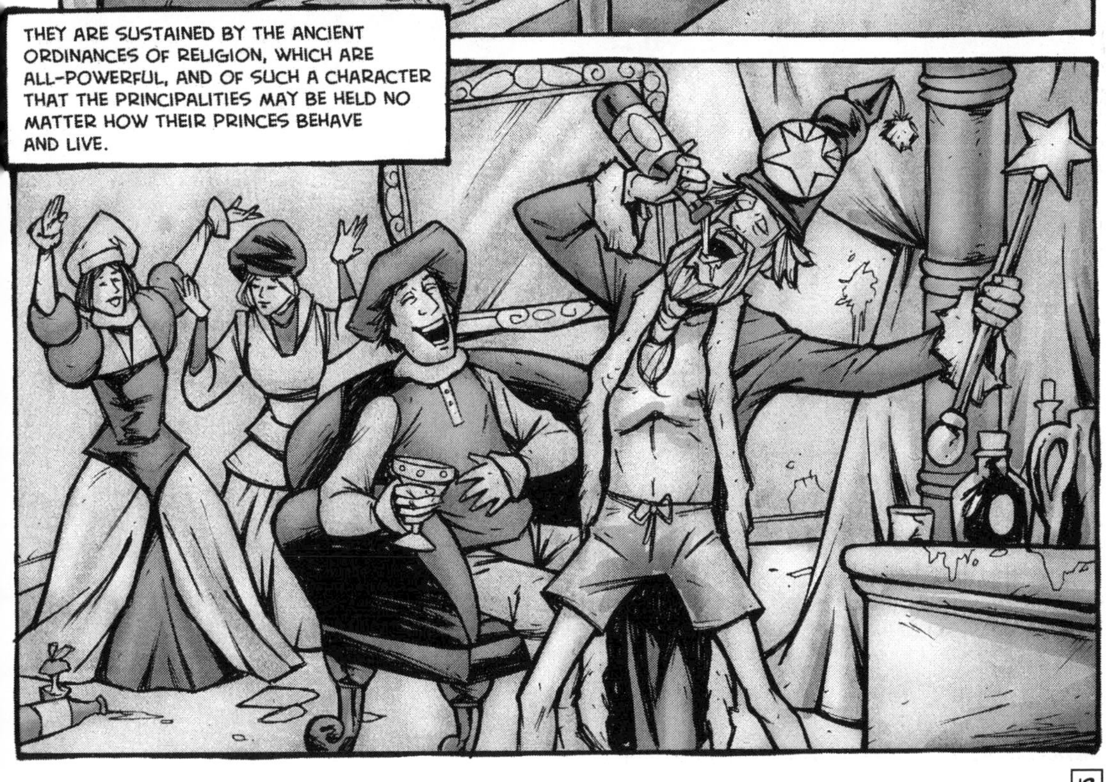
THEY ARE SUSTAINED BY THE ANCIENT ORDINANCES OF RELIGION, WHICH ARE ALL-POWERFUL, AND OF SUCH A CHARACTER THAT THE PRINCIPALITIES MAY BE HELD NO MATTER HOW THEIR PRINCES BEHAVE AND LIVE.

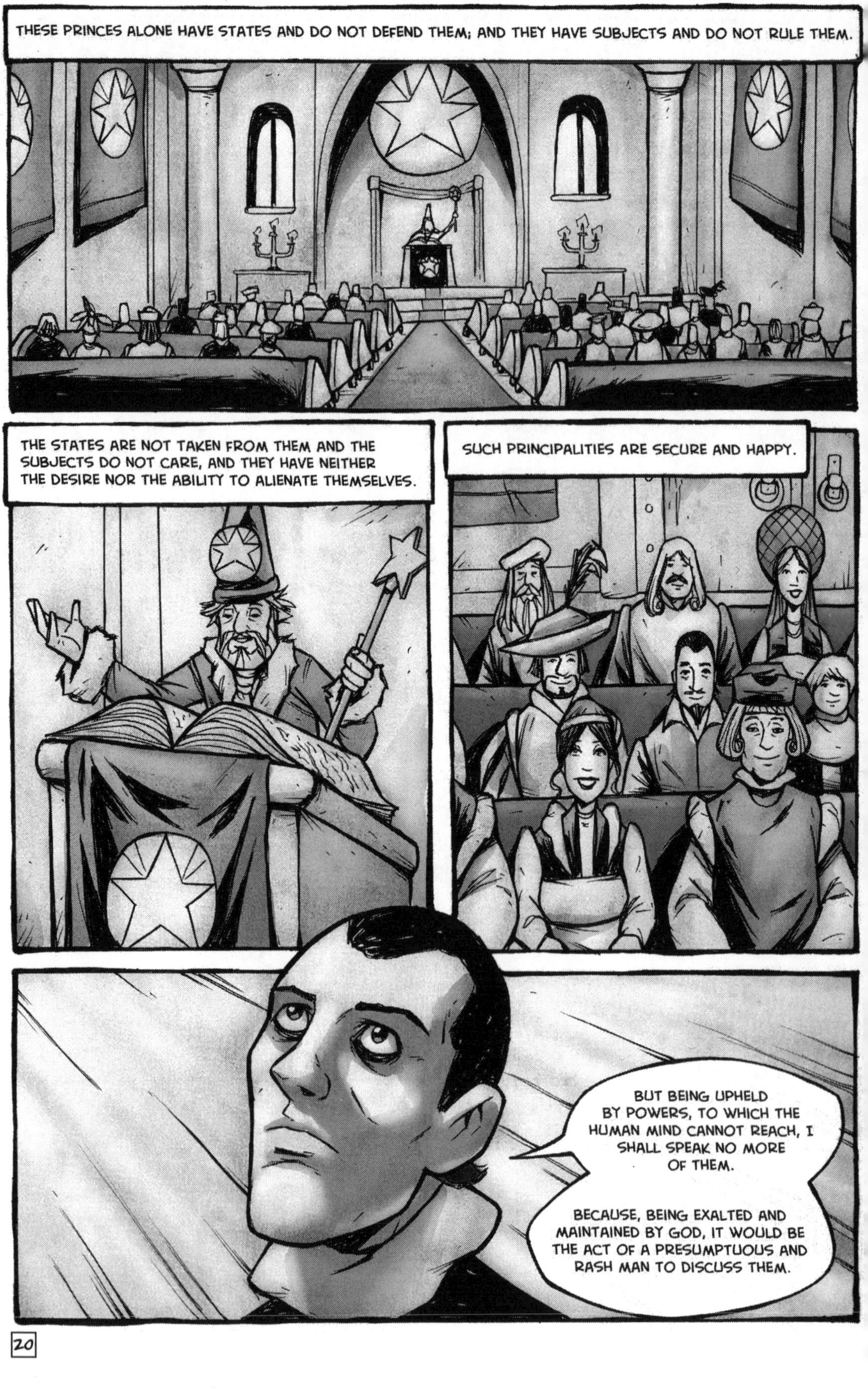

THESE PRINCES ALONE HAVE STATES AND DO NOT DEFEND THEM; AND THEY HAVE SUBJECTS AND DO NOT RULE THEM.
THE STATES ARE NOT TAKEN FROM THEM AND THE SUBJECTS DO NOT CARE, AND THEY HAVE NEITHER THE DESIRE NOR THE ABILITY TO ALIENATE THEMSELVES.
SUCH PRINCIPALITIES ARE SECURE AND HAPPY.
BUT BEING UPHELD BY POWERS, TO WHICH THE HUMAN MIND CANNOT REACH, I SHALL SPEAK NO MORE OF THEM.
BECAUSE, BEING EXALTED AND MAINTAINED BY GOD, IT WOULD BE THE ACT OF A PRESUMPTUOUS AND RASH MAN TO DISCUSS THEM.

HOW MANY KINDS OF SOLDIERY THERE ARE AND CONCERNING MERCENARIES

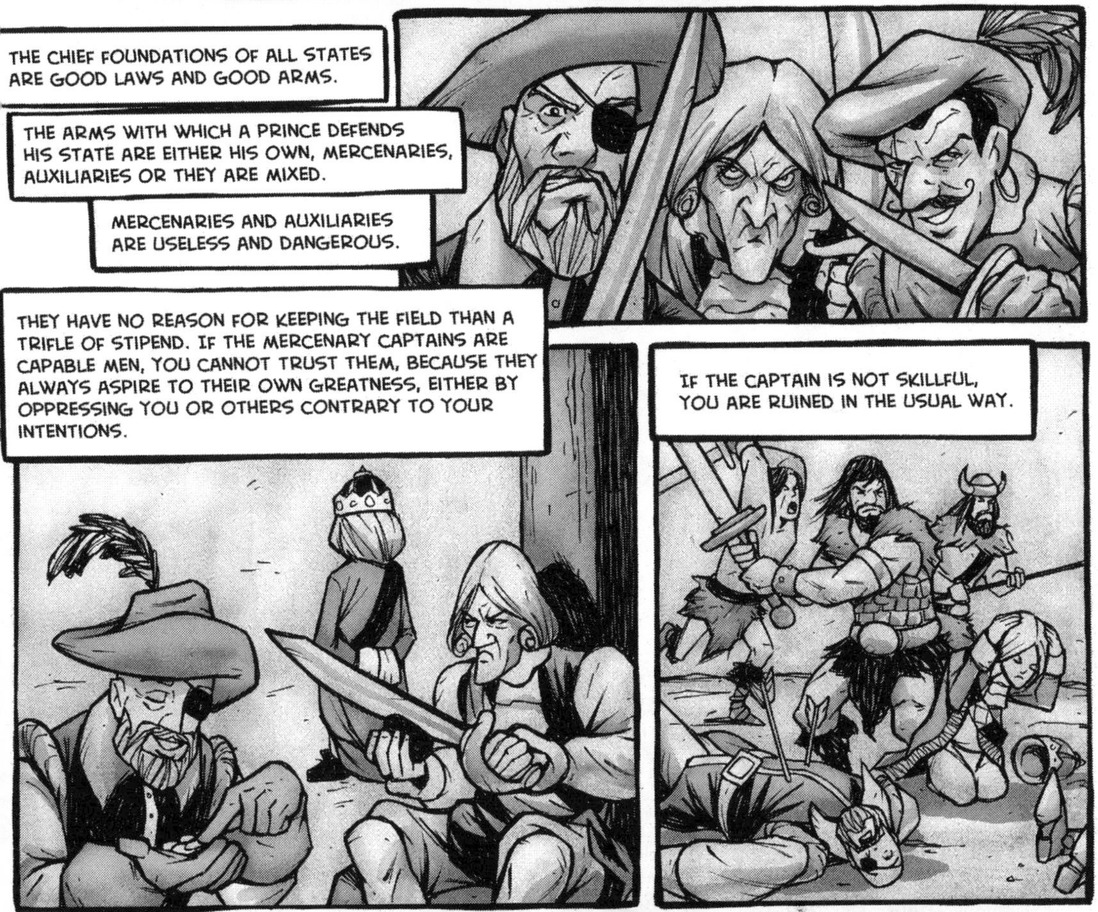
THE CHIEF FOUNDATIONS OF ALL STATES ARE GOOD LAWS AND GOOD ARMS.
THE ARMS WITH WHICH A PRINCE DEFENDS HIS STATE ARE EITHER HIS OWN, MERCENARIES, AUXILIARIES OR THEY ARE MIXED.
MERCENARIES AND AUXILIARIES ARE USELESS AND DANGEROUS.
THEY HAVE NO REASON FOR KEEPING THE FIELD THAN A TRIFLE OF STIPEND. IF THE MERCENARY CAPTAINS ARE CAPABLE MEN, YOU CANNOT TRUST THEM, BECAUSE THEY ALWAYS ASPIRE TO THEIR OWN GREATNESS, EITHER BY OPPRESSING YOU OR OTHERS CONTRARY TO YOUR INTENTIONS.
IF THE CAPTAIN IS NOT SKILLFUL, YOU ARE RUINED IN THE USUAL WAY.

CONCERNING AUXILIARIES, MIXED SOLDIERY, AND ONE'S OWN

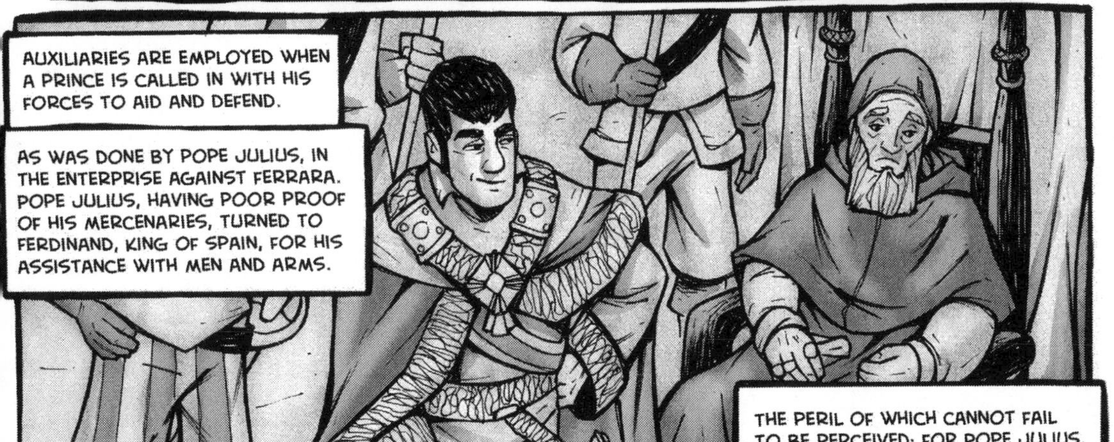
AUXILIARIES ARE EMPLOYED WHEN A PRINCE IS CALLED IN WITH HIS FORCES TO AID AND DEFEND.
AS WAS DONE BY POPE JULIUS, IN THE ENTERPRISE AGAINST FERRARA. POPE JULIUS, HAVING POOR PROOF OF HIS MERCENARIES, TURNED TO FERDINAND, KING OF SPAIN, FOR HIS ASSISTANCE WITH MEN AND ARMS.
THE PERIL OF WHICH CANNOT FAIL TO BE PERCEIVED; FOR POPE JULIUS, WISHING TO GET FERRARA, THREW HIMSELF ENTIRELY INTO THE HANDS OF THE FOREIGNER.

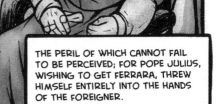

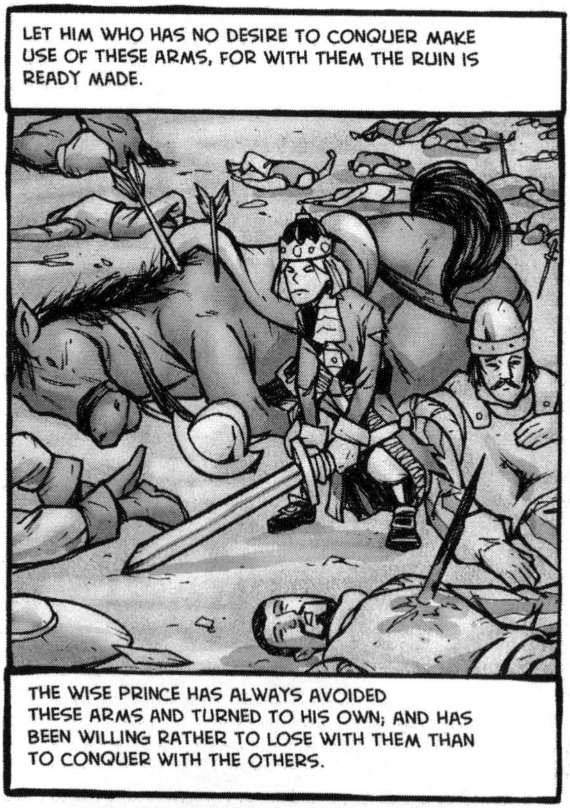
LET HIM WHO HAS NO DESIRE TO CONQUER MAKE USE OF THESE ARMS, FOR WITH THEM THE RUIN IS READY MADE.
THE WISE PRINCE HAS ALWAYS AVOIDED THESE ARMS AND TURNED TO HIS OWN; AND HAS BEEN WILLING RATHER TO LOSE WITH THEM THAN TO CONQUER WITH THE OTHERS.

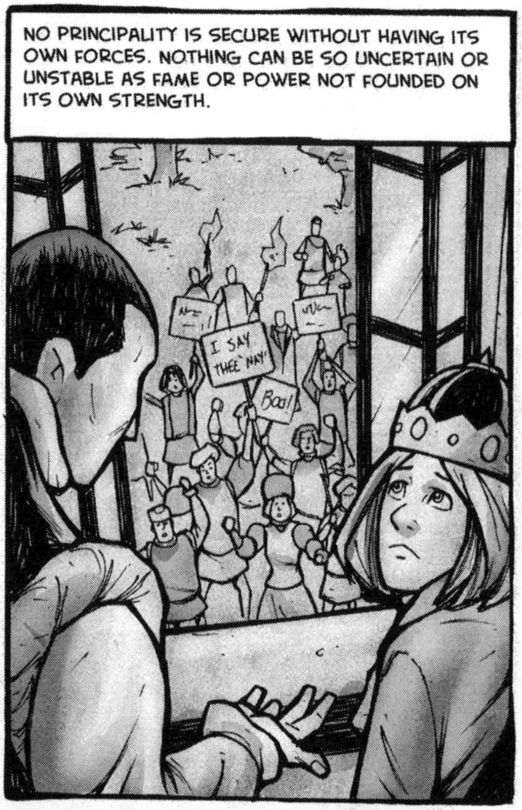
NO PRINCIPALITY IS SECURE WITHOUT HAVING ITS OWN FORCES. NOTHING CAN BE SO UNCERTAIN OR UNSTABLE AS FAME OR POWER NOT FOUNDED ON ITS OWN STRENGTH.
I SAY THEE `NAY'
Boo!

THAT WHICH CONCERNS A PRINCE ON THE SUBJECT OF THE ART OF WAR

A PRINCE OUGHT TO HAVE NO OTHER AIM OR THOUGHT, THAN WAR AND ITS RULES AND DISCIPLINE. IT IS SEEN THAT WHEN PRINCES HAVE THOUGHT MORE OF EASE THAN OF ARMS THEY HAVE LOST THEIR STATES.

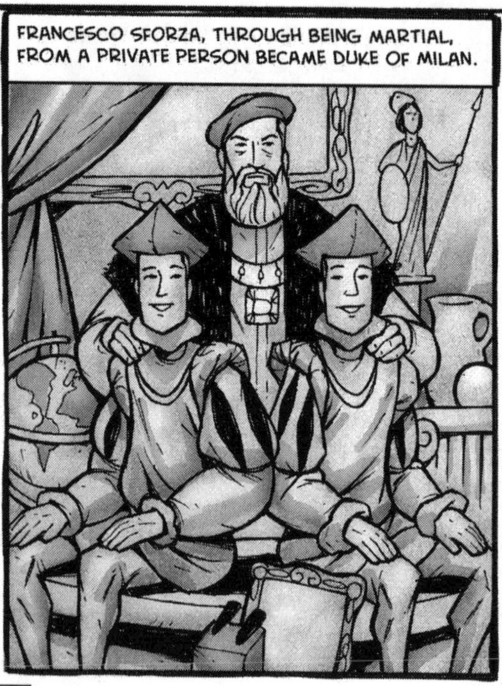
FRANCESCO SFORZA, THROUGH BEING MARTIAL, FROM A PRIVATE PERSON BECAME DUKE OF MILAN.

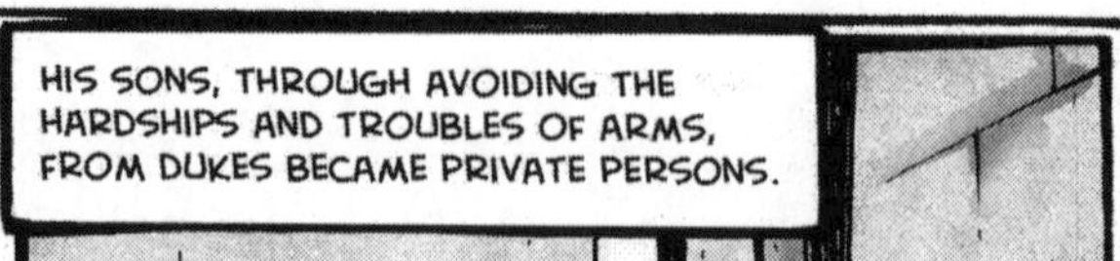
HIS SONS, THROUGH AVOIDING THE HARDSHIPS AND TROUBLES OF ARMS, FROM DUKES BECAME PRIVATE PERSONS.

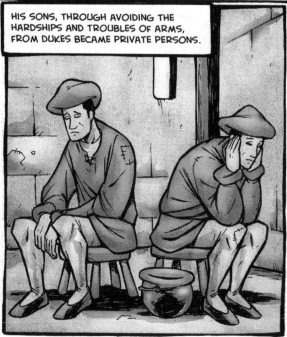

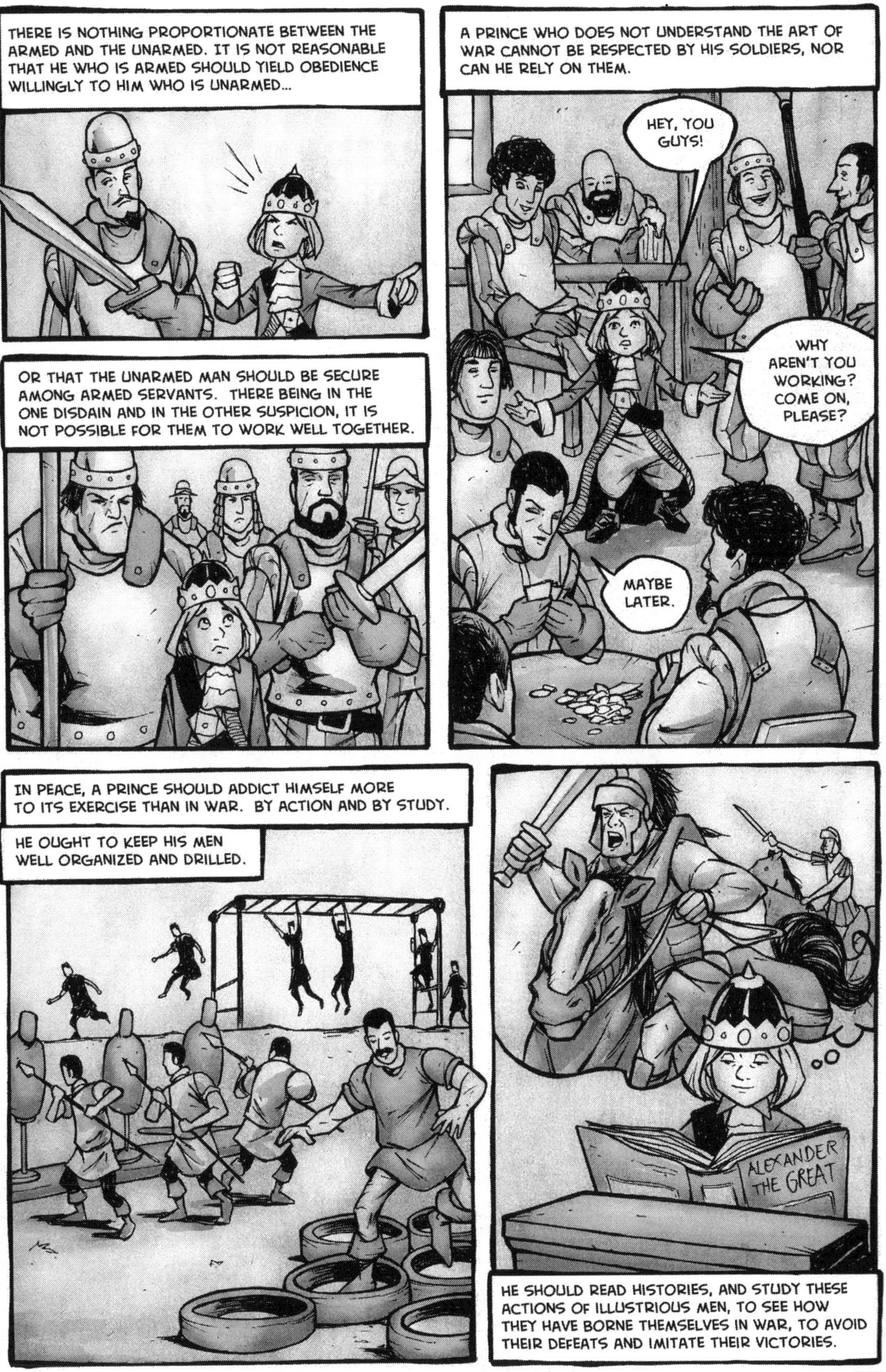
THERE IS NOTHING PROPORTIONATE BETWEEN THE ARMED AND THE UNARMED. IT IS NOT REASONABLE THAT HE WHO IS ARMED SHOULD YIELD OBEDIENCE WILLINGLY TO HIM WHO IS UNARMED...
A PRINCE WHO DOES NOT UNDERSTAND THE ART OF WAR CANNOT BE RESPECTED BY HIS SOLDIERS, NOR CAN HE RELY ON THEM.
HEY, YOU GUYS!
WHY AREN'T YOU WORKING? COME ON, PLEASE?
MAYBE LATER.
OR THAT THE UNARMED MAN SHOULD BE SECURE AMONG ARMED SERVANTS. THERE BEING IN THE ONE DISDAIN AND IN THE OTHER SUSPICION, IT IS NOT POSSIBLE FOR THEM TO WORK WELL TOGETHER.
IN PEACE, A PRINCE SHOULD ADDICT HIMSELF MORE TO ITS EXERCISE THAN IN WAR. BY ACTION AND BY STUDY.
HE OUGHT TO KEEP HIS MEN WELL ORGANIZED AND DRILLED.
ALEXANDER THE GREAT
HE SHOULD READ HISTORIES, AND STUDY THESE ACTIONS OF ILLUSTRIOUS MEN, TO SEE HOW THEY HAVE BORNE THEMSELVES IN WAR, TO AVOID THEIR DEFEATS AND IMITATE THEIR VICTORIES.

CONCERNING THINGS FOR WHICH MEN, AND ESPECIALLY PRINCES, ARE PRAISED OR BLAMED

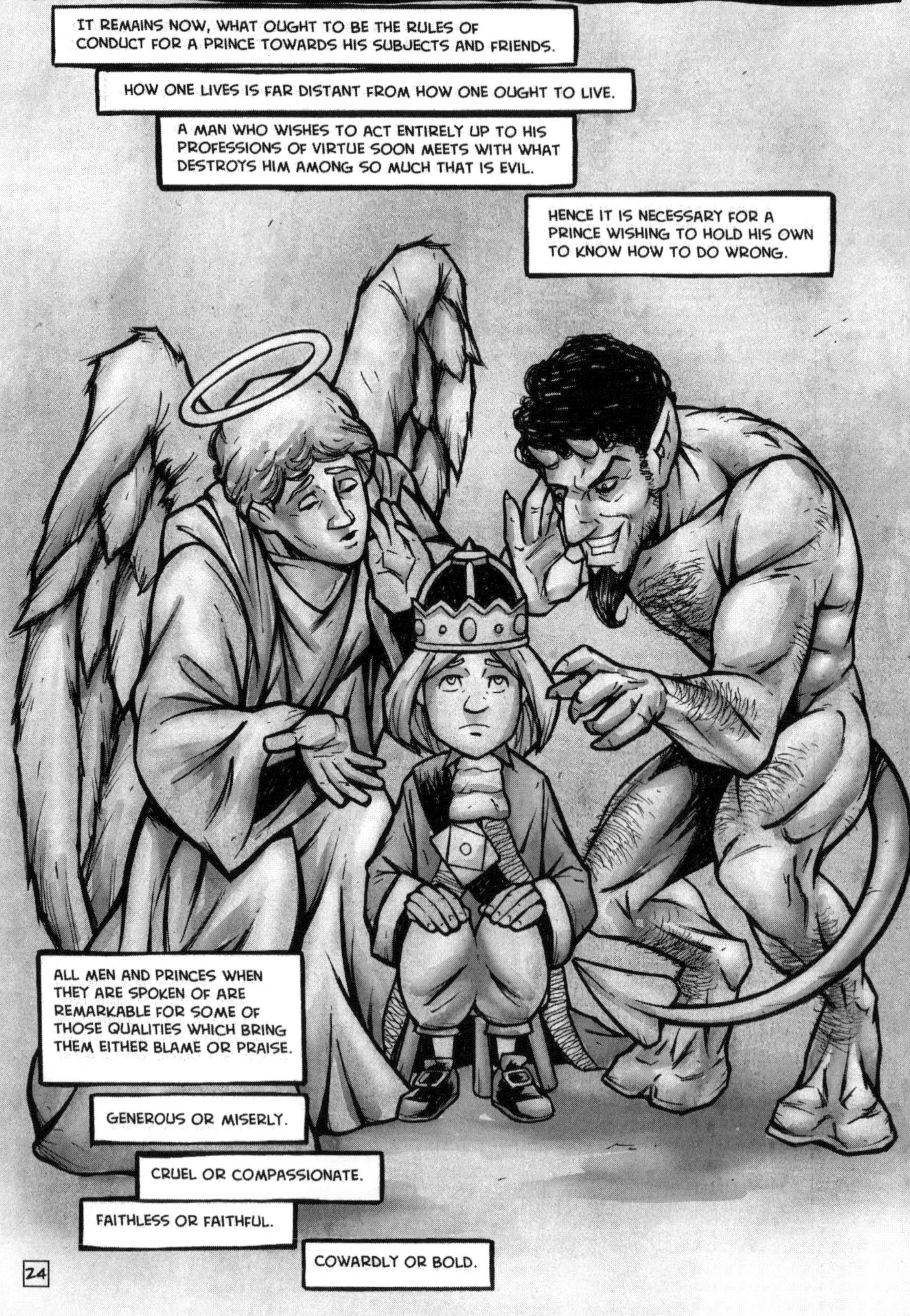
IT REMAINS NOW, WHAT OUGHT TO BE THE RULES OF CONDUCT FOR A PRINCE TOWARDS HIS SUBJECTS AND FRIENDS.
HOW ONE LIVES IS FAR DISTANT FROM HOW ONE OUGHT TO LIVE.
A MAN WHO WISHES TO ACT ENTIRELY UP TO HIS PROFESSIONS OF VIRTUE SOON MEETS WITH WHAT DESTROYS HIM AMONG SO MUCH THAT IS EVIL.
HENCE IT IS NECESSARY FOR A PRINCE WISHING TO HOLD HIS OWN TO KNOW HOW TO DO WRONG.
ALL MEN AND PRINCES WHEN THEY ARE SPOKEN OF ARE REMARKABLE FOR SOME OF THOSE QUALITIES WHICH BRING THEM EITHER BLAME OR PRAISE.
GENEROUS OR MISERLY.
CRUEL OR COMPASSIONATE.
FAITHLESS OR FAITHFUL.
COWARDLY OR BOLD.

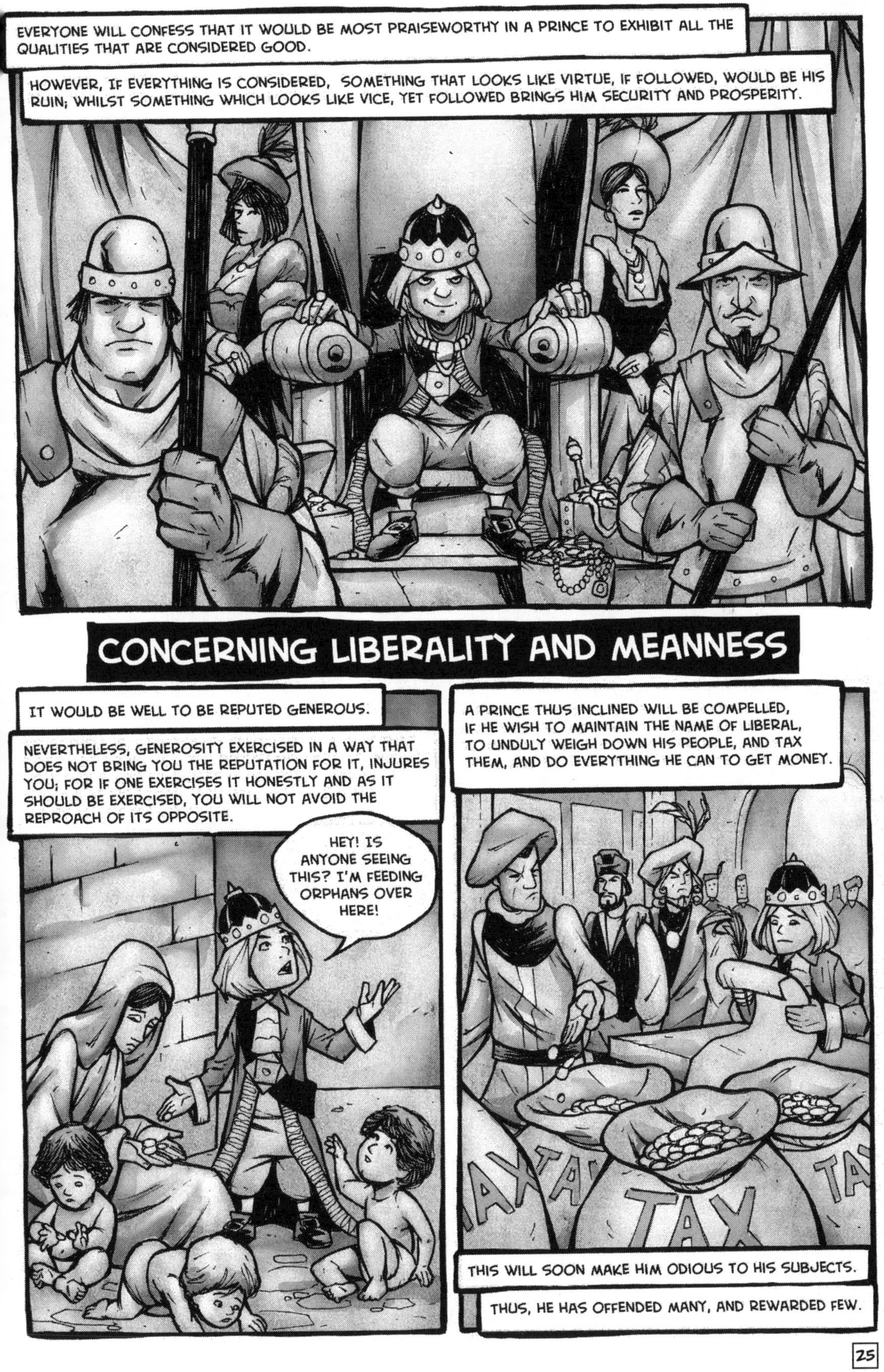
EVERYONE WILL CONFESS THAT IT WOULD BE MOST PRAISEWORTHY IN A PRINCE TO EXHIBIT ALL THE QUALITIES THAT ARE CONSIDERED GOOD.
HOWEVER, IF EVERYTHING IS CONSIDERED, SOMETHING THAT LOOKS LIKE VIRTUE, IF FOLLOWED, WOULD BE HIS RUIN; WHILST SOMETHING WHICH LOOKS LIKE VICE, YET FOLLOWED BRINGS HIM SECURITY AND PROSPERITY.
CONCERNING LIBERALITY AND MEANNESS
IT WOULD BE WELL TO BE REPUTED GENEROUS.
NEVERTHELESS, GENEROSITY EXERCISED IN A WAY THAT DOES NOT BRING YOU THE REPUTATION FOR IT, INJURES YOU; FOR IF ONE EXERCISES IT HONESTLY AND AS IT SHOULD BE EXERCISED, YOU WILL NOT AVOID THE REPROACH OF ITS OPPOSITE.
HEY! IS ANYONE SEEING THIS? I'M FEEDING ORPHANS OVER HERE!
A PRINCE THUS INCLINED WILL BE COMPELLED, IF HE WISH TO MAINTAIN THE NAME OF LIBERAL, TO UNDULY WEIGH DOWN HIS PEOPLE, AND TAX THEM, AND DO EVERYTHING HE CAN TO GET MONEY.
TAX
THIS WILL SOON MAKE HIM ODIOUS TO HIS SUBJECTS.
THUS, HE HAS OFFENDED MANY, AND REWARDED FEW.

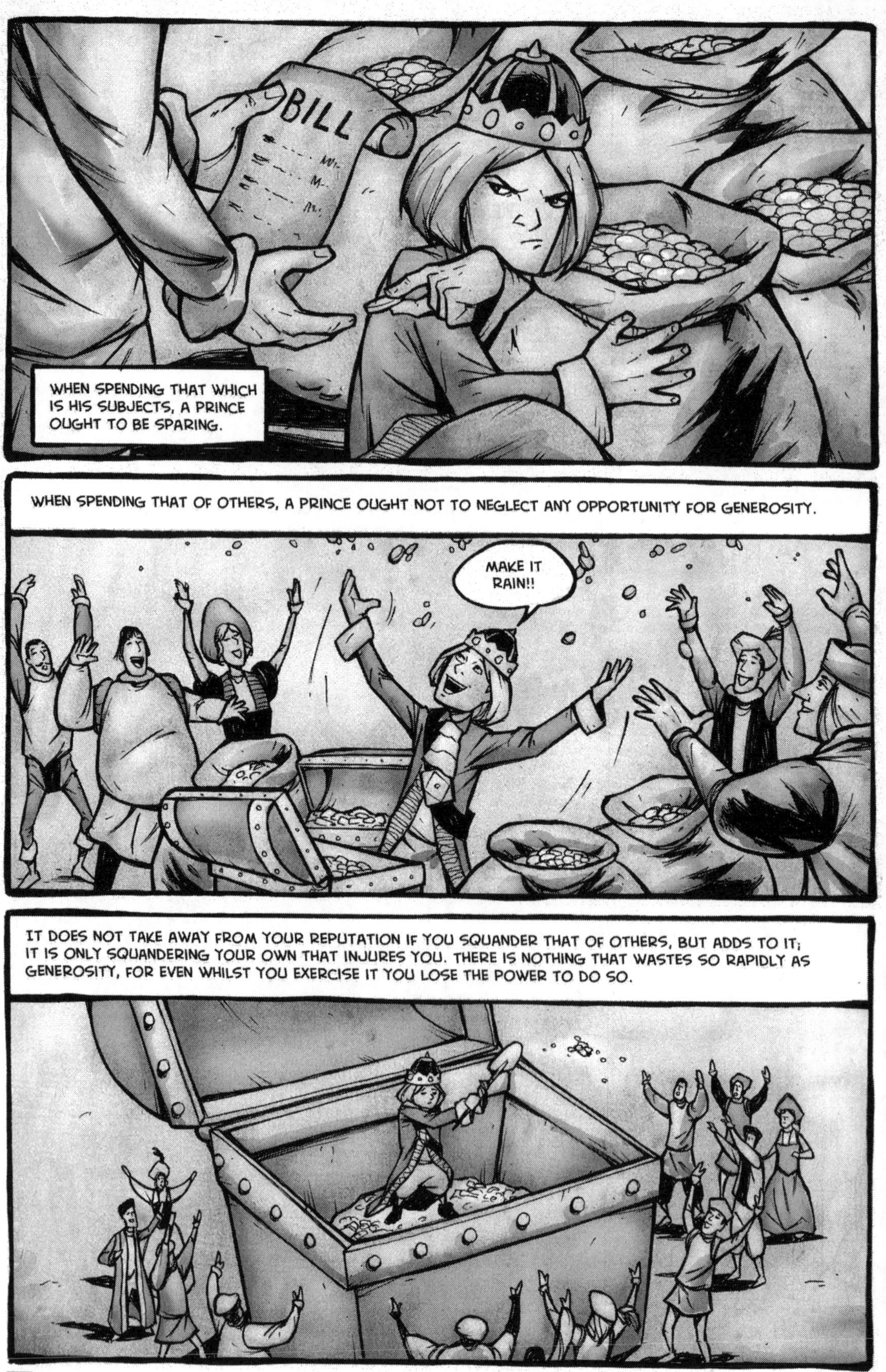
BILL
WHEN SPENDING THAT WHICH IS HIS SUBJECTS, A PRINCE OUGHT TO BE SPARING.
WHEN SPENDING THAT OF OTHERS, A PRINCE OUGHT NOT TO NEGLECT ANY OPPORTUNITY FOR GENEROSITY.
MAKE IT RAIN!!
IT DOES NOT TAKE AWAY FROM YOUR REPUTATION IF YOU SQUANDER THAT OF OTHERS, BUT ADDS TO IT; IT IS ONLY SQUANDERING YOUR OWN THAT INJURES YOU. THERE IS NOTHING THAT WASTES SO RAPIDLY AS GENEROSITY, FOR EVEN WHILST YOU EXERCISE IT YOU LOSE THE POWER TO DO SO.

CONCERNING CRUELTY AND CLEMENCY, AND WHETHER IT IS BETTER TO BE LOVED THAN FEARED

EVERY PRINCE OUGHT TO DESIRE TO BE CONSIDERED CLEMENT AND NOT CRUEL. NEVERTHELESS HE OUGHT TO TAKE CARE NOT TO MISUSE THIS CLEMENCY.

CESARE BORGIA WAS CONSIDERED CRUEL; NOTWITHSTANDING, HIS CRUELTY RECONCILED ROMAGNA, UNIFIED IT, AND RESTORED IT TO PEACE.

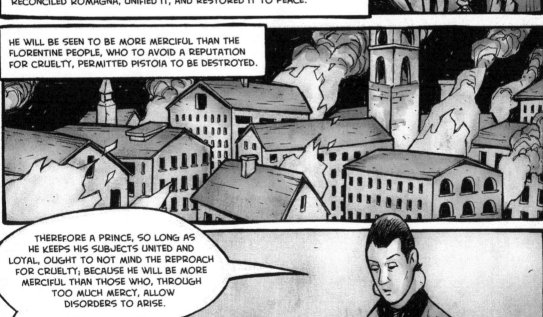

HE WILL BE SEEN TO BE MORE MERCIFUL THAN THE FLORENTINE PEOPLE, WHO TO AVOID A REPUTATION FOR CRUELTY, PERMITTED PISTOIA TO BE DESTROYED.

THEREFORE A PRINCE, SO LONG AS HE KEEPS HIS SUBJECTS UNITED AND LOYAL, OUGHT TO NOT MIND THE REPROACH FOR CRUELTY; BECAUSE HE WILL BE MORE MERCIFUL THAN THOSE WHO, THROUGH TOO MUCH MERCY, ALLOW DISORDERS TO ARISE.

A PRINCE OUGHT TO BE SLOW TO BELIEVE AND TO ACT, NOR SHOULD HE SHOW FEAR, BUT PROCEED IN A TEMPERATE MANNER WITH PRUDENCE AND HUMANITY.

UPON THIS A QUESTION ARISES: WHETHER IT IS BETTER TO BE LOVED THAN FEARED OR FEARED THAN LOVED?

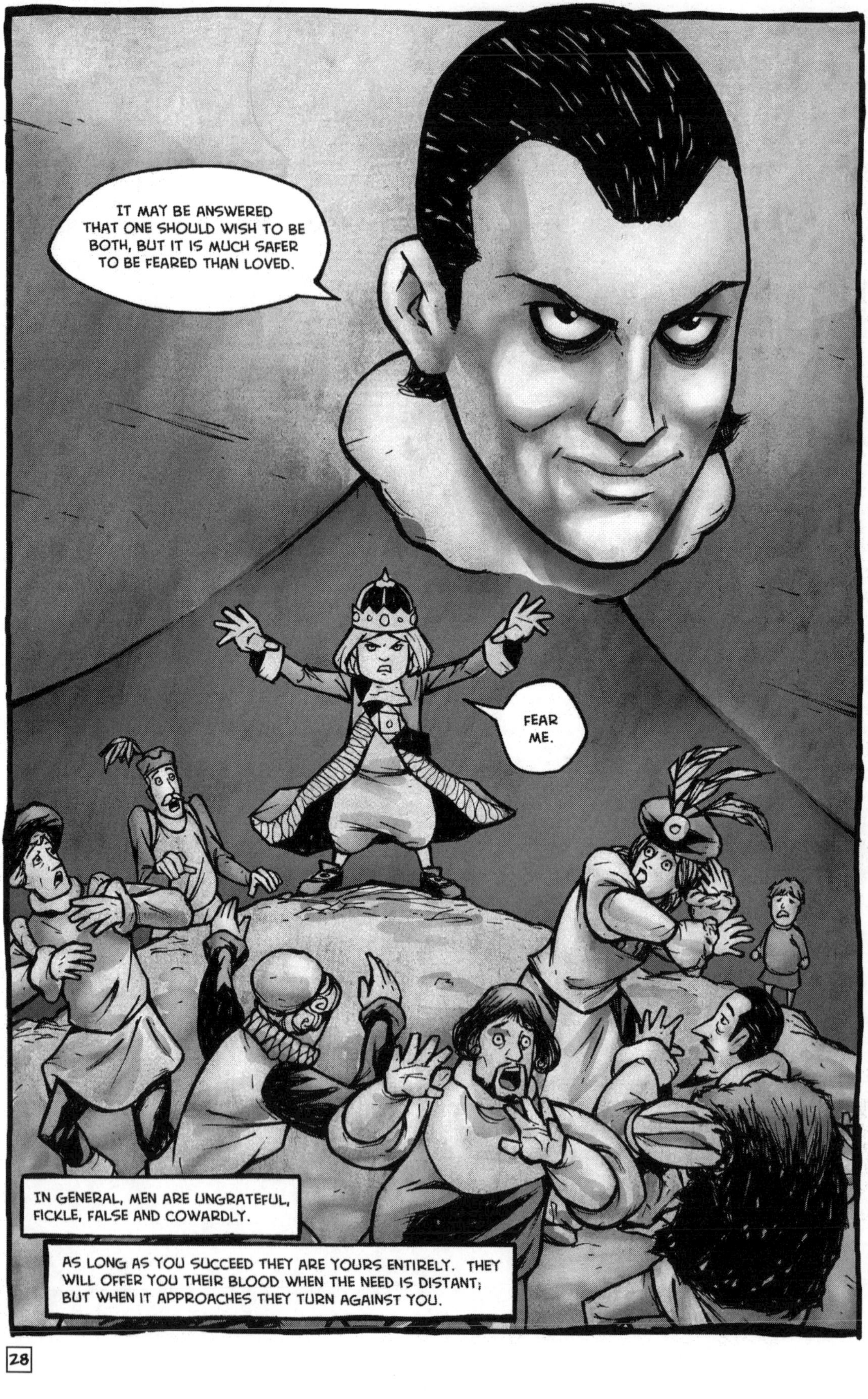
IT MAY BE ANSWERED THAT ONE SHOULD WISH TO BE BOTH, BUT IT IS MUCH SAFER TO BE FEARED THAN LOVED.
FEAR ME.
IN GENERAL, MEN ARE UNGRATEFUL, FICKLE, FALSE AND COWARDLY.
AS LONG AS YOU SUCCEED THEY ARE YOURS ENTIRELY. THEY WILL OFFER YOU THEIR BLOOD WHEN THE NEED IS DISTANT; BUT WHEN IT APPROACHES THEY TURN AGAINST YOU.

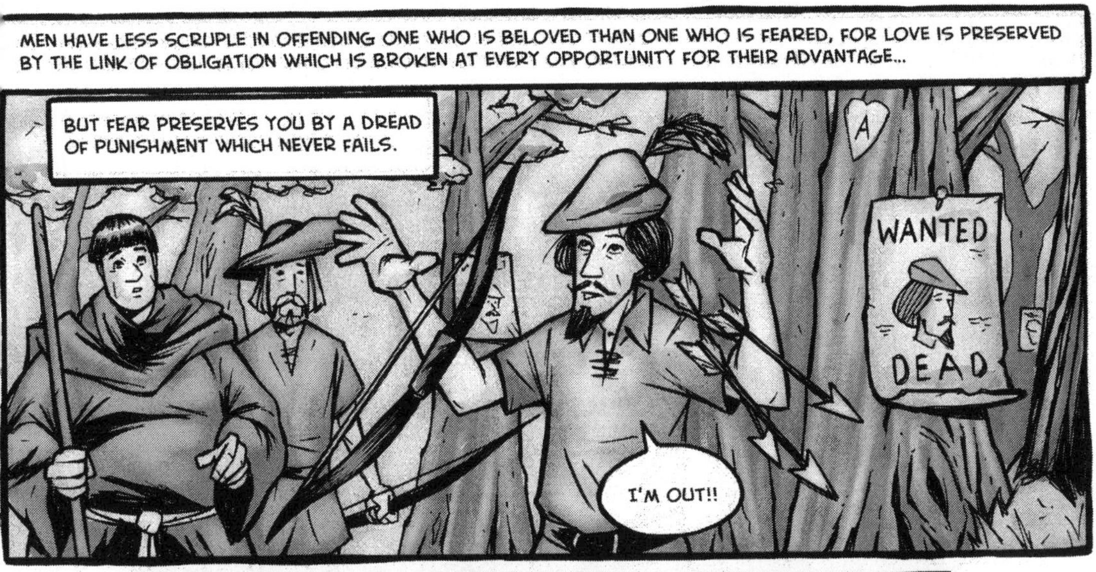
MEN HAVE LESS SCRUPLE IN OFFENDING ONE WHO IS BELOVED THAN ONE WHO IS FEARED, FOR LOVE IS PRESERVED BY THE LINK OF OBLIGATION WHICH IS BROKEN AT EVERY OPPORTUNITY FOR THEIR ADVANTAGE...
BUT FEAR PRESERVES YOU BY A DREAD OF PUNISHMENT WHICH NEVER FAILS.
A
WANTED
DEAD
I'M OUT!!

CONCERNING THE WAY IN WHICH PRINCES SHOULD KEEP FAITH

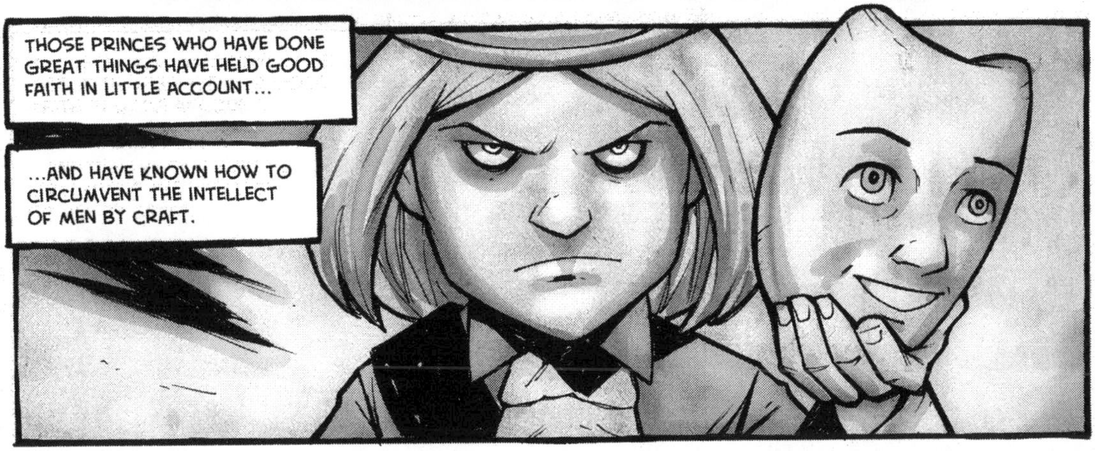
THOSE PRINCES WHO HAVE DONE GREAT THINGS HAVE HELD GOOD FAITH IN LITTLE ACCOUNT...
...AND HAVE KNOWN HOW TO CIRCUMVENT THE INTELLECT OF MEN BY CRAFT.

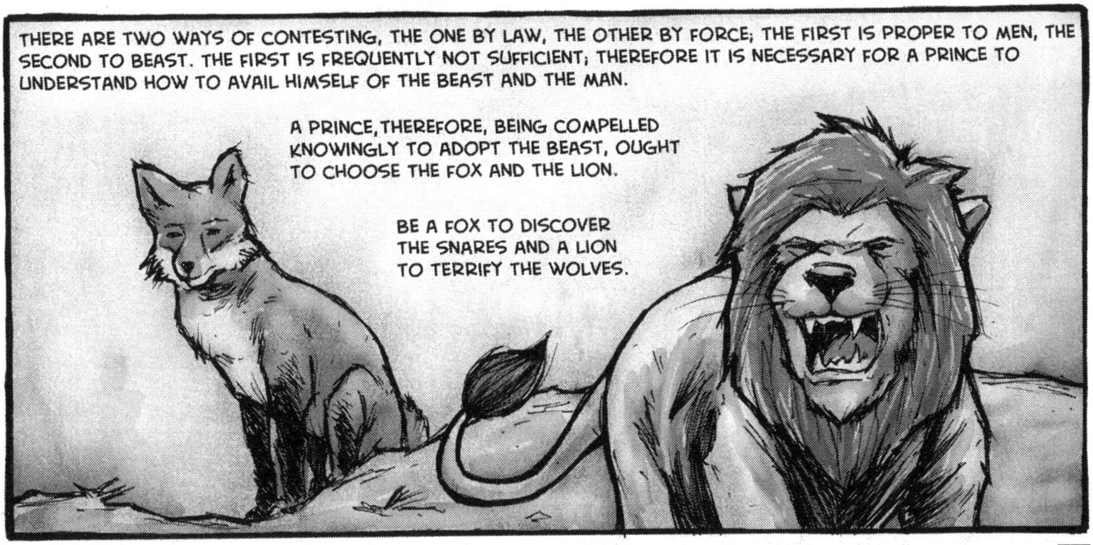
THERE ARE TWO WAYS OF CONTESTING, THE ONE BY LAW, THE OTHER BY FORCE; THE FIRST IS PROPER TO MEN, THE SECOND TO BEAST. THE FIRST IS FREQUENTLY NOT SUFFICIENT; THEREFORE IT IS NECESSARY FOR A PRINCE TO UNDERSTAND HOW TO AVAIL HIMSELF OF THE BEAST AND THE MAN.
A PRINCE, THEREFORE, BEING COMPELLED KNOWINGLY TO ADOPT THE BEAST, OUGHT TO CHOOSE THE FOX AND THE LION.
BE A FOX TO DISCOVER THE SNARES AND A LION TO TERRIFY THE WOLVES.

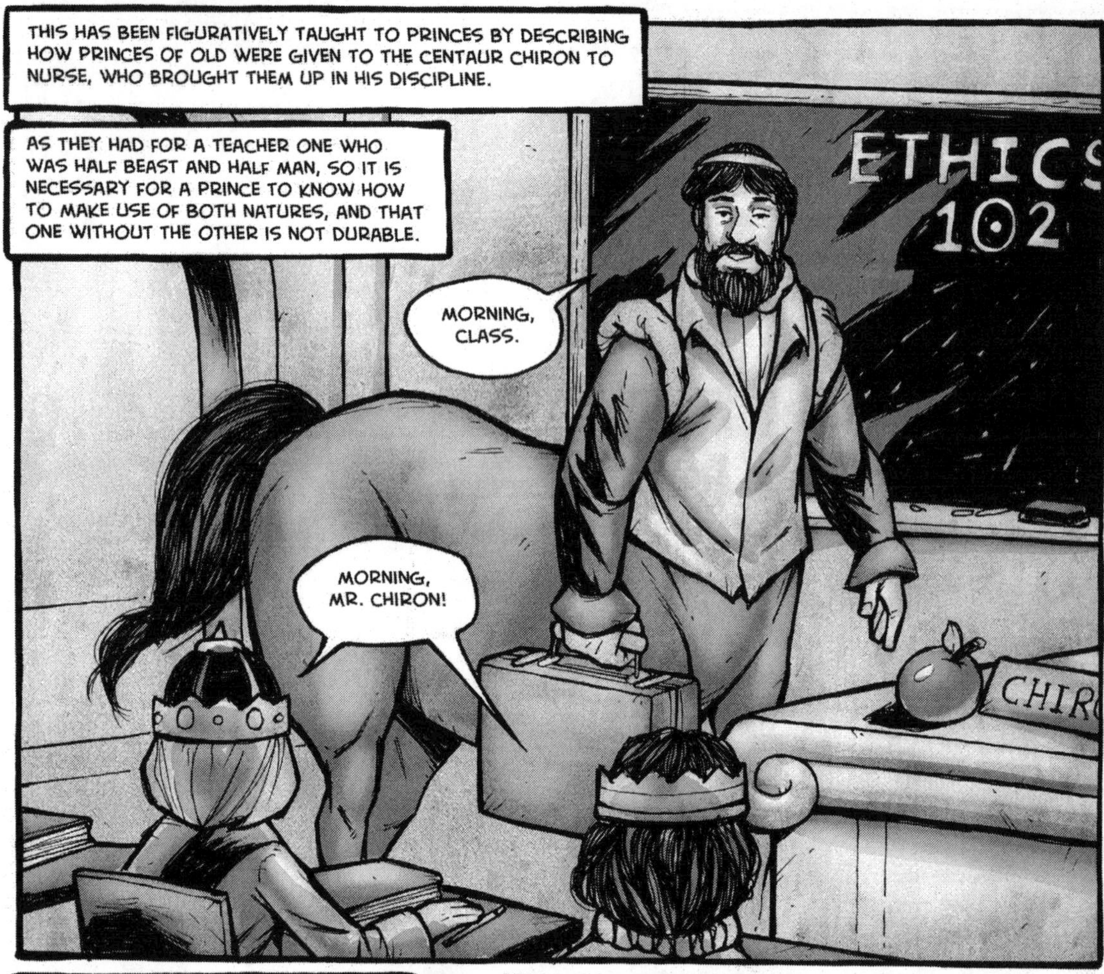
THIS HAS BEEN FIGURATIVELY TAUGHT TO PRINCES BY DESCRIBING HOW PRINCES OF OLD WERE GIVEN TO THE CENTAUR CHIRON TO NURSE, WHO BROUGHT THEM UP IN HIS DISCIPLINE.
AS THEY HAD FOR A TEACHER ONE WHO WAS HALF BEAST AND HALF MAN, SO IT IS NECESSARY FOR A PRINCE TO KNOW HOW TO MAKE USE OF BOTH NATURES, AND THAT ONE WITHOUT THE OTHER IS NOT DURABLE.
ETHICS 102
MORNING, CLASS.
MORNING, MR. CHIRON!

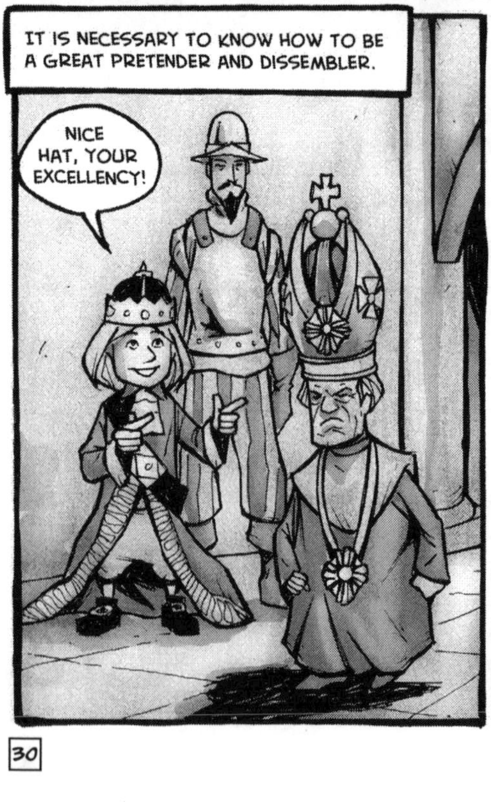
IT IS NECESSARY TO KNOW HOW TO BE A GREAT PRETENDER AND DISSEMBLER.
NICE HAT, YOUR EXCELLENCY!

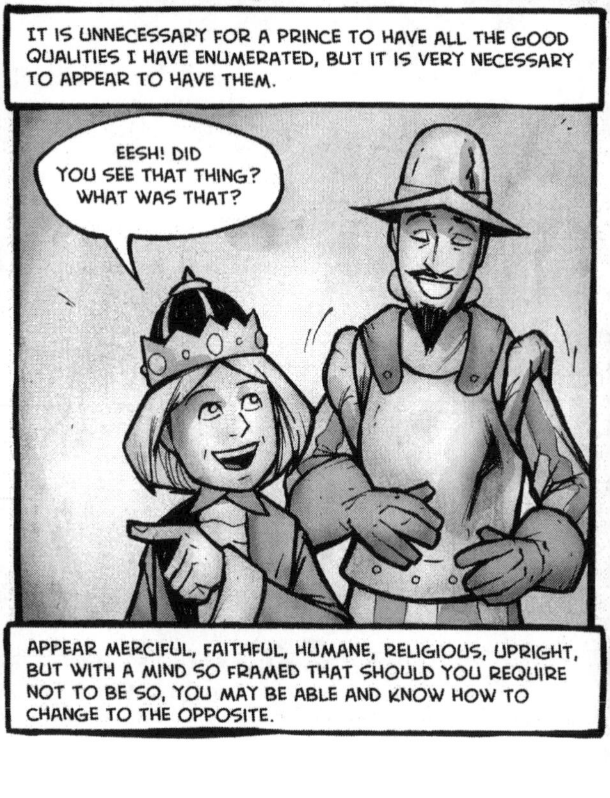
IT IS UNNECESSARY FOR A PRINCE TO HAVE ALL THE GOOD QUALITIES I HAVE ENUMERATED, BUT IT IS VERY NECESSARY TO APPEAR TO HAVE THEM.
EESH! DID YOU SEE THAT THING? WHAT WAS THAT?
APPEAR MERCIFUL, FAITHFUL, HUMANE, RELIGIOUS, UPRIGHT, BUT WITH A MIND SO FRAMED THAT SHOULD YOU REQUIRE NOT TO BE SO, YOU MAY BE ABLE AND KNOW HOW TO CHANGE TO THE OPPOSITE.

THAT ONE SHOULD AVOID BEING DESPISED AND HATED

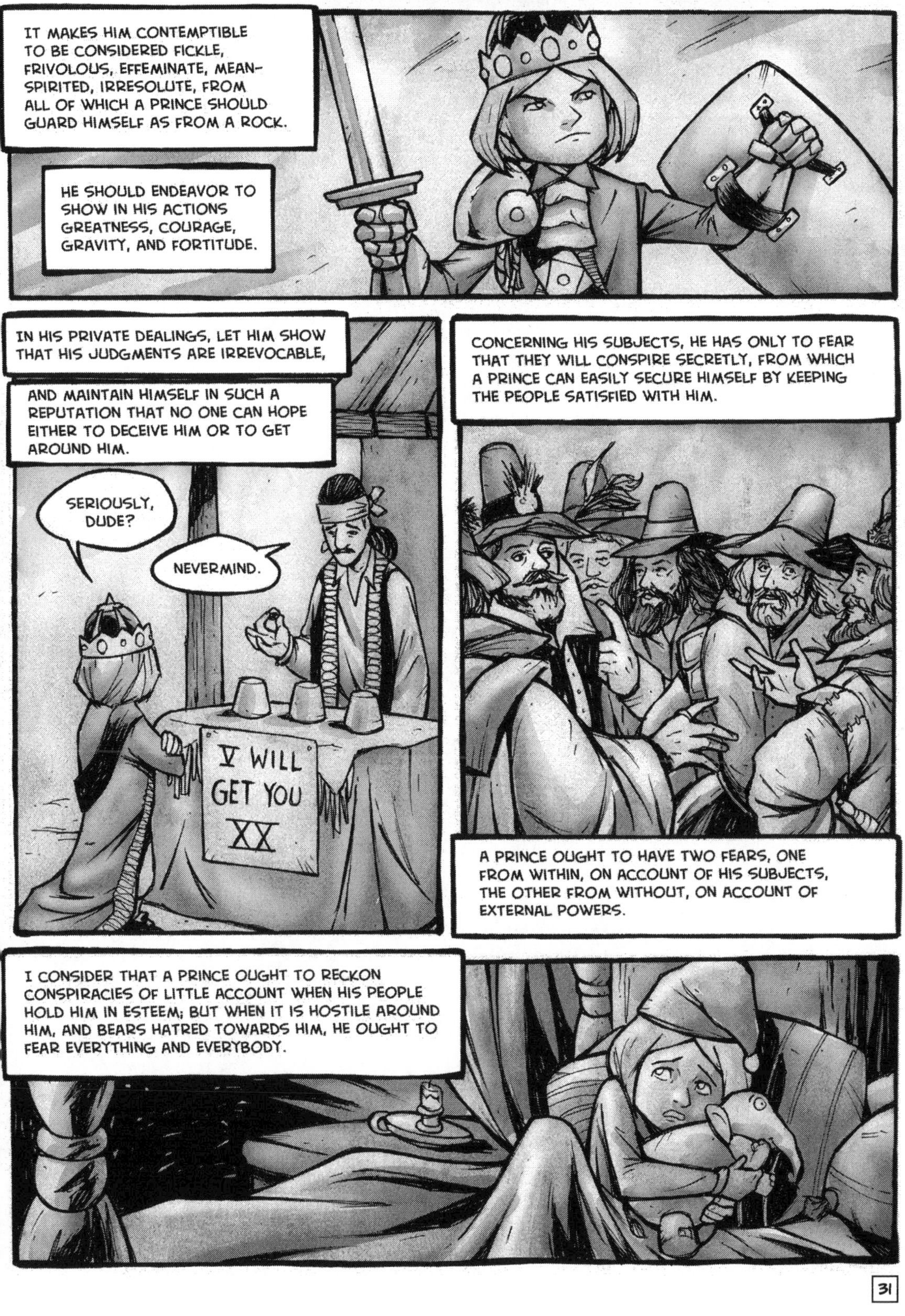
IT MAKES HIM CONTEMPTIBLE TO BE CONSIDERED FICKLE, FRIVOLOUS, EFFEMINATE, MEAN-SPIRITED, IRRESOLUTE, FROM ALL OF WHICH A PRINCE SHOULD GUARD HIMSELF AS FROM A ROCK.
HE SHOULD ENDEAVOR TO SHOW IN HIS ACTIONS GREATNESS, COURAGE, GRAVITY, AND FORTITUDE.
IN HIS PRIVATE DEALINGS, LET HIM SHOW THAT HIS JUDGMENTS ARE IRREVOCABLE,
AND MAINTAIN HIMSELF IN SUCH A REPUTATION THAT NO ONE CAN HOPE EITHER TO DECEIVE HIM OR TO GET AROUND HIM.
SERIOUSLY, DUDE?
NEVERMIND.
V WILL GET YOU XX
CONCERNING HIS SUBJECTS, HE HAS ONLY TO FEAR THAT THEY WILL CONSPIRE SECRETLY, FROM WHICH A PRINCE CAN EASILY SECURE HIMSELF BY KEEPING THE PEOPLE SATISFIED WITH HIM.
A PRINCE OUGHT TO HAVE TWO FEARS, ONE FROM WITHIN, ON ACCOUNT OF HIS SUBJECTS, THE OTHER FROM WITHOUT, ON ACCOUNT OF EXTERNAL POWERS.
I CONSIDER THAT A PRINCE OUGHT TO RECKON CONSPIRACIES OF LITTLE ACCOUNT WHEN HIS PEOPLE HOLD HIM IN ESTEEM; BUT WHEN IT IS HOSTILE AROUND HIM, AND BEARS HATRED TOWARDS HIM, HE OUGHT TO FEAR EVERYTHING AND EVERYBODY.

ARE FORTRESSES, AND MANY OTHER THINGS TO WHICH PRINCES OFTEN RESORT, ADVANTAGEOUS OR HURTFUL?

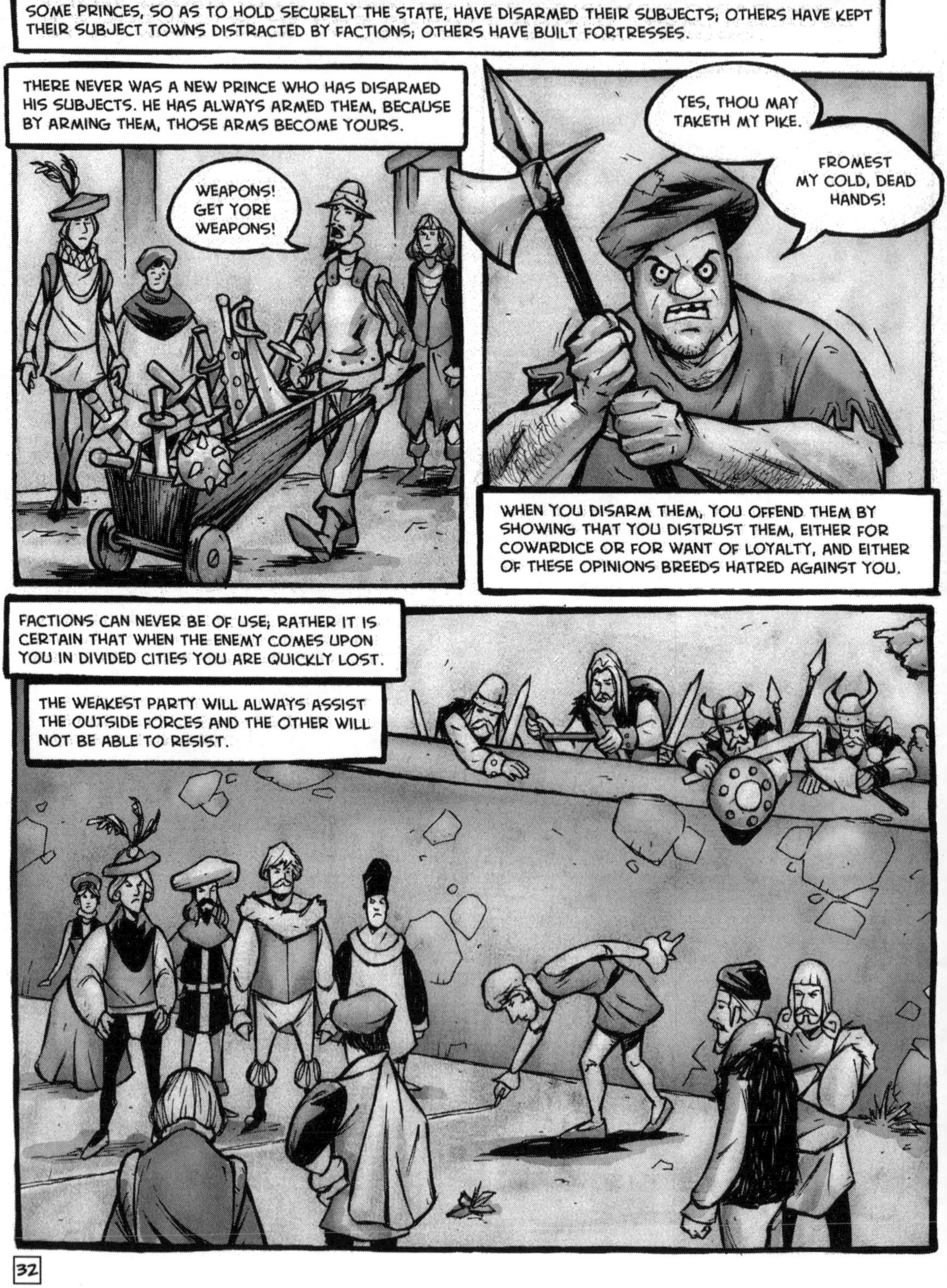
SOME PRINCES, SO AS TO HOLD SECURELY THE STATE, HAVE DISARMED THEIR SUBJECTS; OTHERS HAVE KEPT THEIR SUBJECT TOWNS DISTRACTED BY FACTIONS; OTHERS HAVE BUILT FORTRESSES.
THERE NEVER WAS A NEW PRINCE WHO HAS DISARMED HIS SUBJECTS. HE HAS ALWAYS ARMED THEM, BECAUSE BY ARMING THEM, THOSE ARMS BECOME YOURS.
WEAPONS! GET YORE WEAPONS!
YES, THOU MAY TAKETH MY PIKE.
FROMEST MY COLD, DEAD HANDS!
WHEN YOU DISARM THEM, YOU OFFEND THEM BY SHOWING THAT YOU DISTRUST THEM, EITHER FOR COWARDICE OR FOR WANT OF LOYALTY, AND EITHER OF THESE OPINIONS BREEDS HATRED AGAINST YOU.
FACTIONS CAN NEVER BE OF USE; RATHER IT IS CERTAIN THAT WHEN THE ENEMY COMES UPON YOU IN DIVIDED CITIES YOU ARE QUICKLY LOST.
THE WEAKEST PARTY WILL ALWAYS ASSIST THE OUTSIDE FORCES AND THE OTHER WILL NOT BE ABLE TO RESIST.

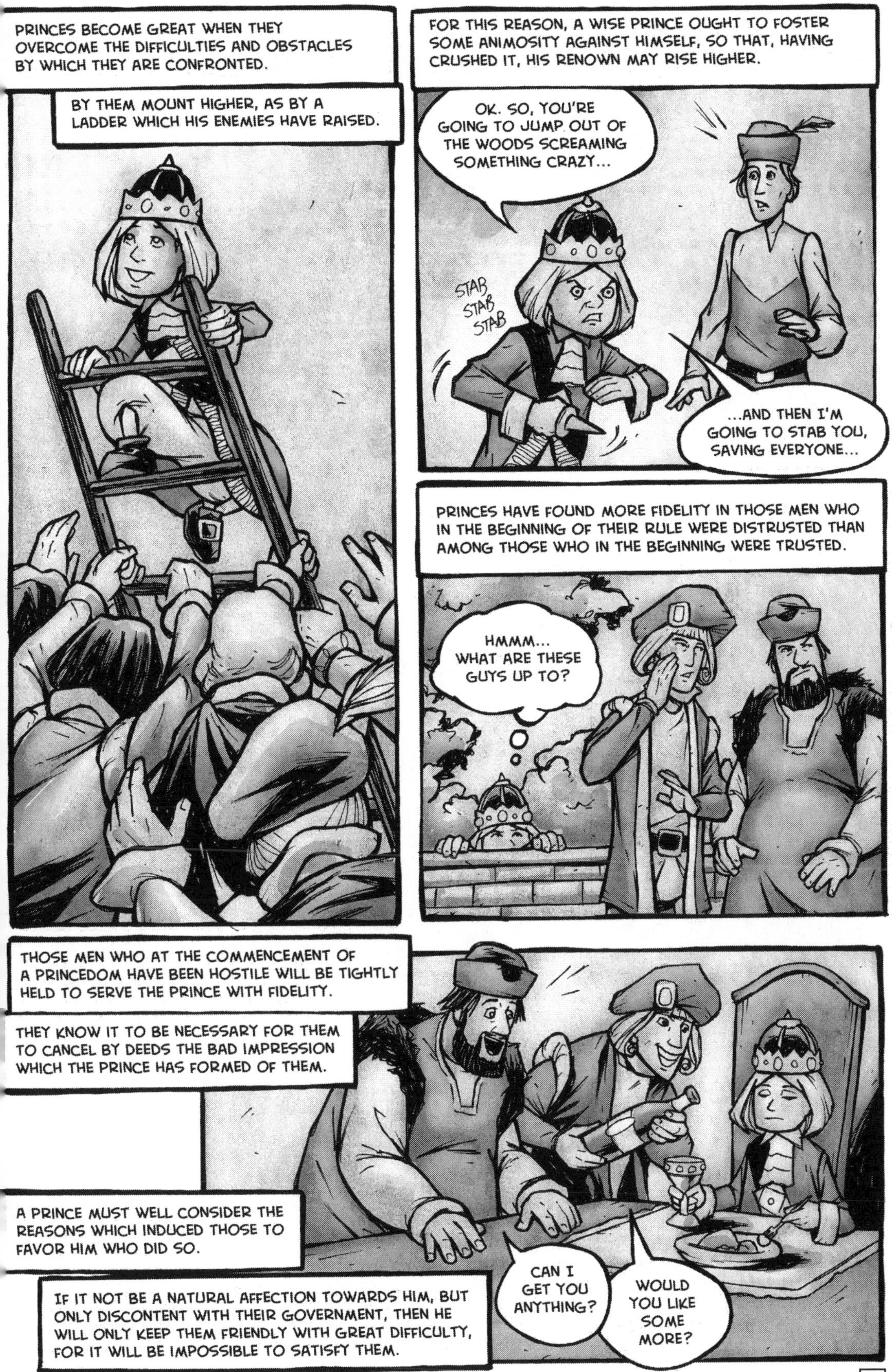
PRINCES BECOME GREAT WHEN THEY OVERCOME THE DIFFICULTIES AND OBSTACLES BY WHICH THEY ARE CONFRONTED.
BY THEM MOUNT HIGHER, AS BY A LADDER WHICH HIS ENEMIES HAVE RAISED.
FOR THIS REASON, A WISE PRINCE OUGHT TO FOSTER SOME ANIMOSITY AGAINST HIMSELF, SO THAT, HAVING CRUSHED IT, HIS RENOWN MAY RISE HIGHER.
OK. SO, YOU'RE GOING TO JUMP OUT OF THE WOODS SCREAMING SOMETHING CRAZY...
STAB STAB STAB
...AND THEN I'M GOING TO STAB YOU, SAVING EVERYONE...
PRINCES HAVE FOUND MORE FIDELITY IN THOSE MEN WHO IN THE BEGINNING OF THEIR RULE WERE DISTRUSTED THAN AMONG THOSE WHO IN THE BEGINNING WERE TRUSTED.
HMMM... WHAT ARE THESE GUYS UP TO?
THOSE MEN WHO AT THE COMMENCEMENT OF A PRINCEDOM HAVE BEEN HOSTILE WILL BE TIGHTLY HELD TO SERVE THE PRINCE WITH FIDELITY.
THEY KNOW IT TO BE NECESSARY FOR THEM TO CANCEL BY DEEDS THE BAD IMPRESSION WHICH THE PRINCE HAS FORMED OF THEM.
A PRINCE MUST WELL CONSIDER THE REASONS WHICH INDUCED THOSE TO FAVOR HIM WHO DID SO.
IF IT NOT BE A NATURAL AFFECTION TOWARDS HIM, BUT ONLY DISCONTENT WITH THEIR GOVERNMENT, THEN HE WILL ONLY KEEP THEM FRIENDLY WITH GREAT DIFFICULTY, FOR IT WILL BE IMPOSSIBLE TO SATISFY THEM.
CAN I GET YOU ANYTHING?
WOULD YOU LIKE SOME MORE?

IT HAS BEEN CUSTOM WITH PRINCES, IN ORDER TO HOLD THEIR STATES MORE SECURELY, TO BUILD FORTRESSES.

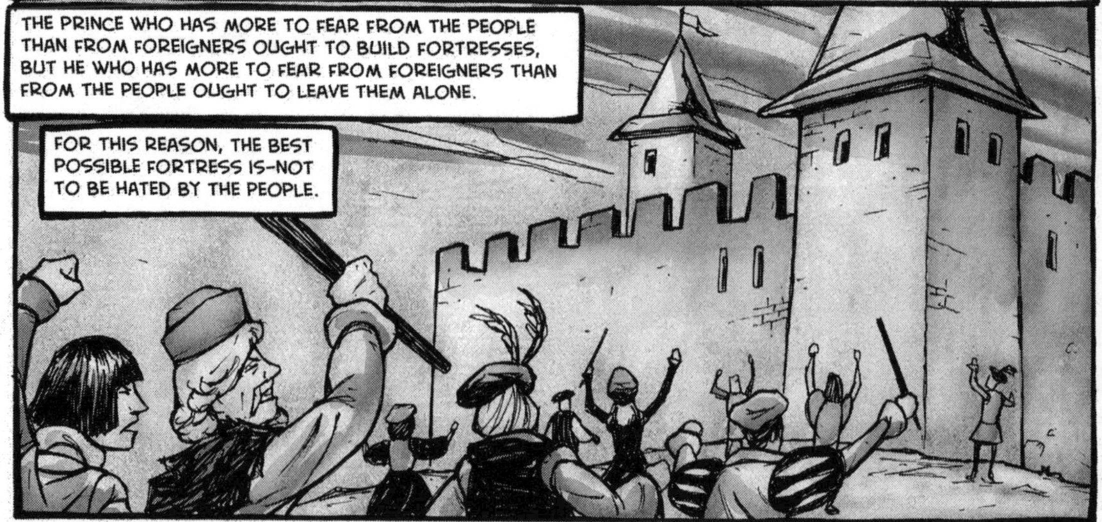
THE PRINCE WHO HAS MORE TO FEAR FROM THE PEOPLE THAN FROM FOREIGNERS OUGHT TO BUILD FORTRESSES, BUT HE WHO HAS MORE TO FEAR FROM FOREIGNERS THAN FROM THE PEOPLE OUGHT TO LEAVE THEM ALONE.
FOR THIS REASON, THE BEST POSSIBLE FORTRESS IS–NOT TO BE HATED BY THE PEOPLE.

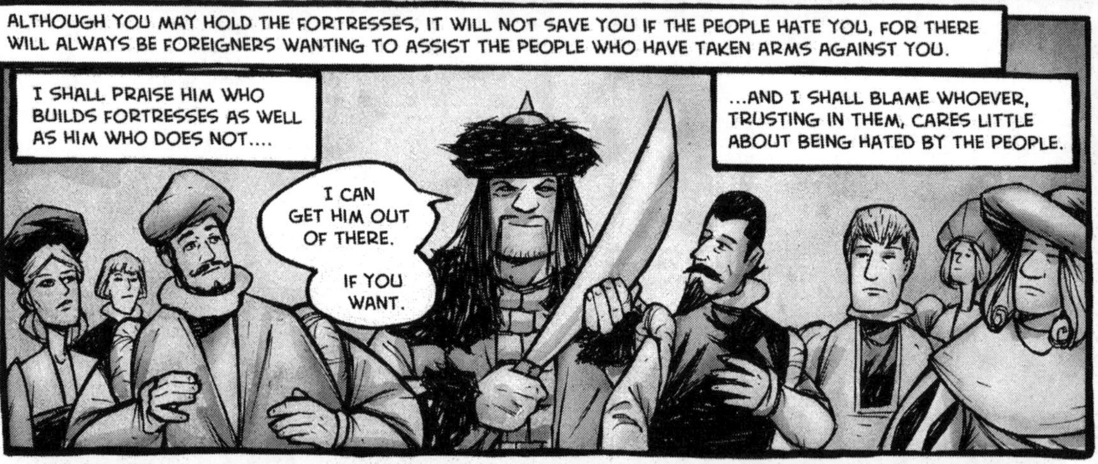
ALTHOUGH YOU MAY HOLD THE FORTRESSES, IT WILL NOT SAVE YOU IF THE PEOPLE HATE YOU, FOR THERE WILL ALWAYS BE FOREIGNERS WANTING TO ASSIST THE PEOPLE WHO HAVE TAKEN ARMS AGAINST YOU.
I SHALL PRAISE HIM WHO BUILDS FORTRESSES AS WELL AS HIM WHO DOES NOT....
I CAN GET HIM OUT OF THERE.
IF YOU WANT.
...AND I SHALL BLAME WHOEVER, TRUSTING IN THEM, CARES LITTLE ABOUT BEING HATED BY THE PEOPLE.

HOW A PRINCE SHOULD CONDUCT HIMSELF SO AS TO GAIN RENOWN

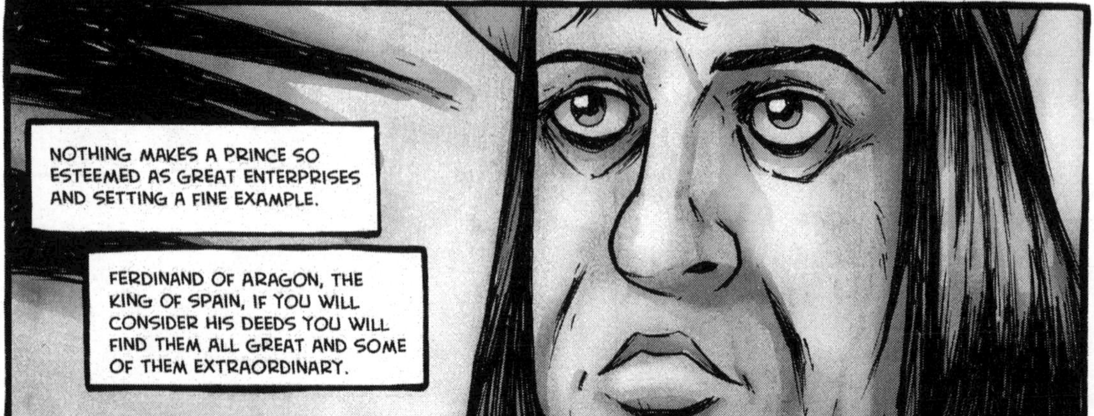
NOTHING MAKES A PRINCE SO ESTEEMED AS GREAT ENTERPRISES AND SETTING A FINE EXAMPLE.
FERDINAND OF ARAGON, THE KING OF SPAIN, IF YOU WILL CONSIDER HIS DEEDS YOU WILL FIND THEM ALL GREAT AND SOME OF THEM EXTRAORDINARY.

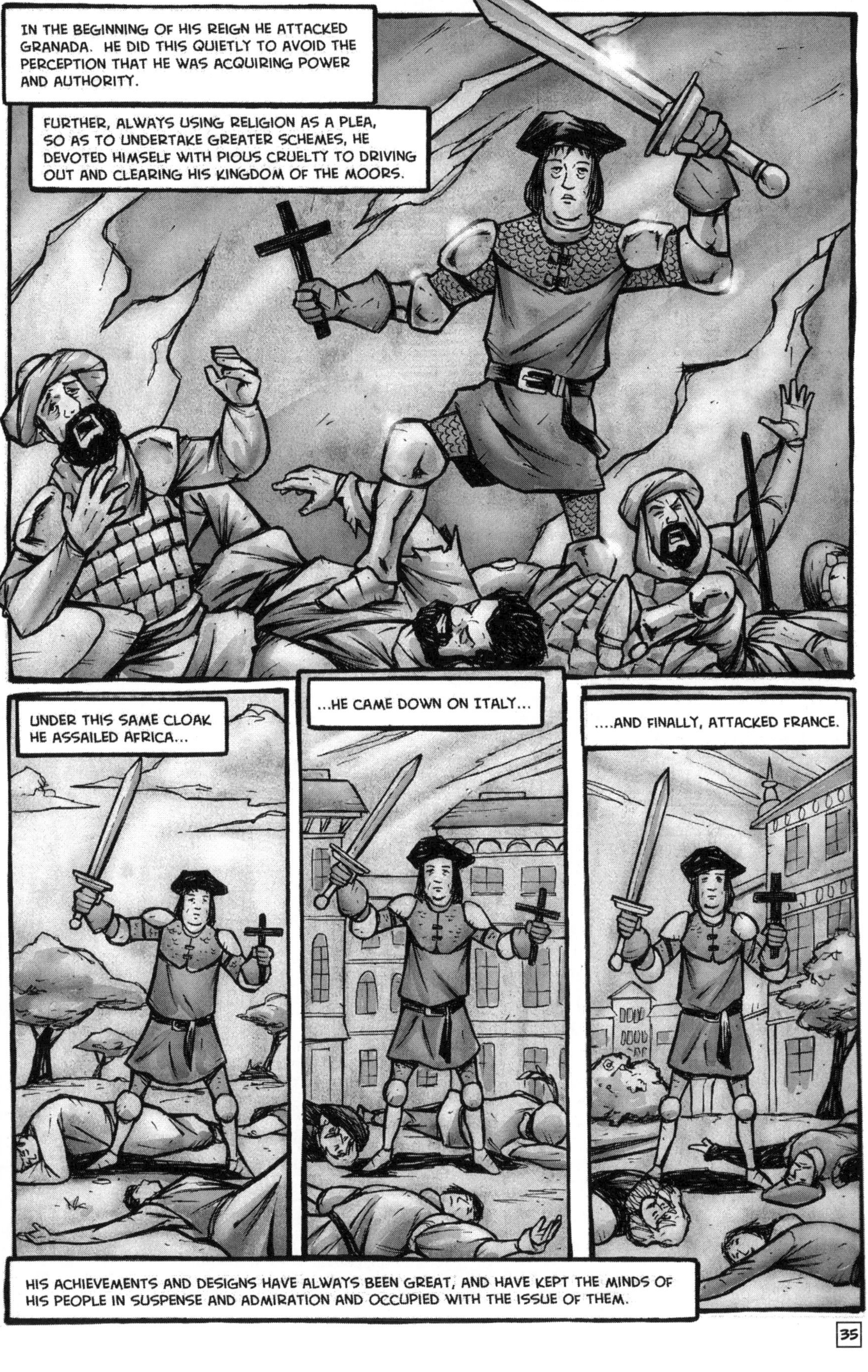

IN THE BEGINNING OF HIS REIGN HE ATTACKED GRANADA. HE DID THIS QUIETLY TO AVOID THE PERCEPTION THAT HE WAS ACQUIRING POWER AND AUTHORITY.
FURTHER, ALWAYS USING RELIGION AS A PLEA, SO AS TO UNDERTAKE GREATER SCHEMES, HE DEVOTED HIMSELF WITH PIOUS CRUELTY TO DRIVING OUT AND CLEARING HIS KINGDOM OF THE MOORS.
UNDER THIS SAME CLOAK HE ASSAILED AFRICA...
...HE CAME DOWN ON ITALY...
....AND FINALLY, ATTACKED FRANCE.
HIS ACHIEVEMENTS AND DESIGNS HAVE ALWAYS BEEN GREAT, AND HAVE KEPT THE MINDS OF HIS PEOPLE IN SUSPENSE AND ADMIRATION AND OCCUPIED WITH THE ISSUE OF THEM.

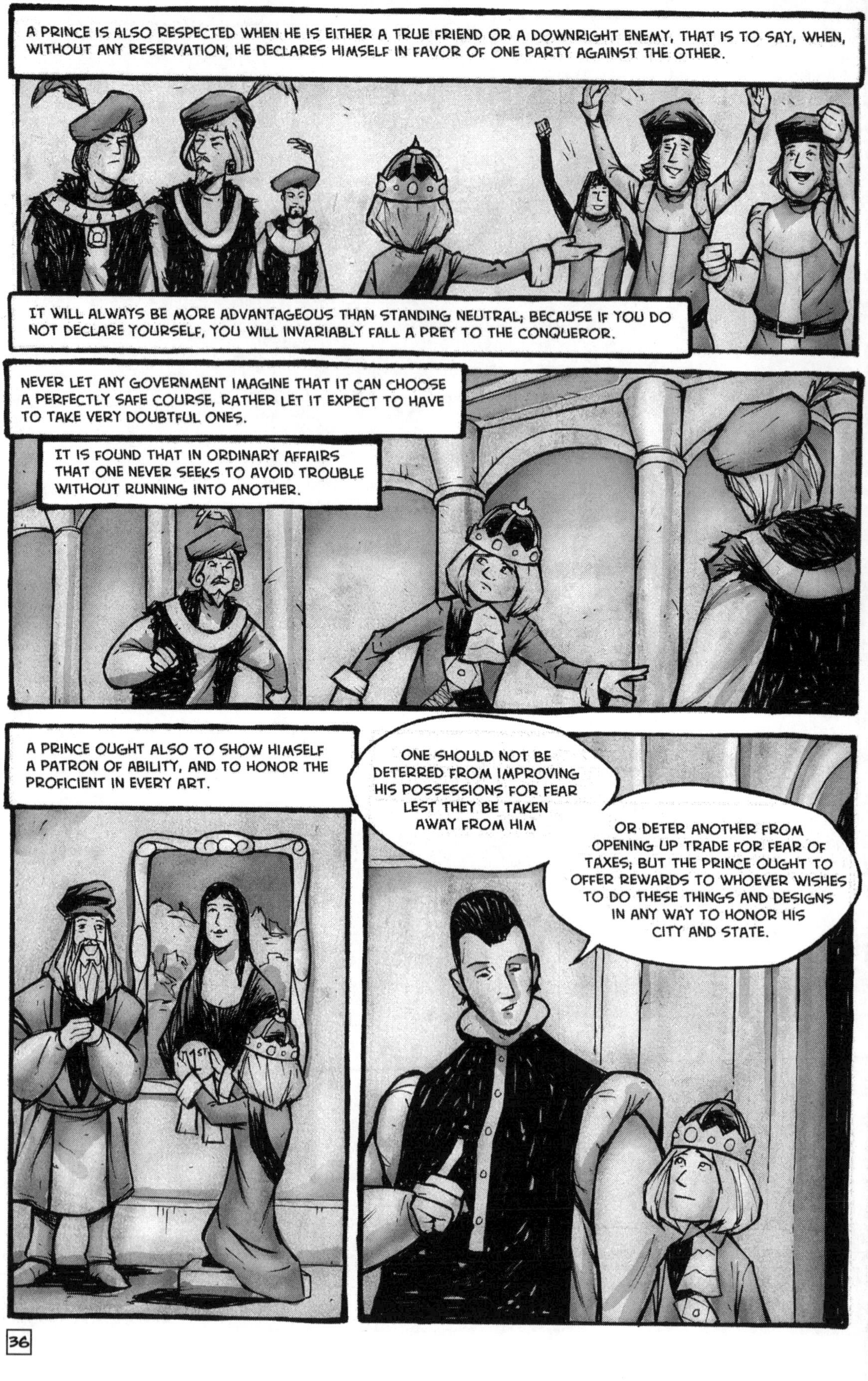
A PRINCE IS ALSO RESPECTED WHEN HE IS EITHER A TRUE FRIEND OR A DOWNRIGHT ENEMY, THAT IS TO SAY, WHEN, WITHOUT ANY RESERVATION, HE DECLARES HIMSELF IN FAVOR OF ONE PARTY AGAINST THE OTHER.
IT WILL ALWAYS BE MORE ADVANTAGEOUS THAN STANDING NEUTRAL; BECAUSE IF YOU DO NOT DECLARE YOURSELF, YOU WILL INVARIABLY FALL A PREY TO THE CONQUEROR.
NEVER LET ANY GOVERNMENT IMAGINE THAT IT CAN CHOOSE A PERFECTLY SAFE COURSE, RATHER LET IT EXPECT TO HAVE TO TAKE VERY DOUBTFUL ONES.
IT IS FOUND THAT IN ORDINARY AFFAIRS THAT ONE NEVER SEEKS TO AVOID TROUBLE WITHOUT RUNNING INTO ANOTHER.
A PRINCE OUGHT ALSO TO SHOW HIMSELF A PATRON OF ABILITY, AND TO HONOR THE PROFICIENT IN EVERY ART.
1ST
ONE SHOULD NOT BE DETERRED FROM IMPROVING HIS POSSESSIONS FOR FEAR LEST THEY BE TAKEN AWAY FROM HIM
OR DETER ANOTHER FROM OPENING UP TRADE FOR FEAR OF TAXES; BUT THE PRINCE OUGHT TO OFFER REWARDS TO WHOEVER WISHES TO DO THESE THINGS AND DESIGNS IN ANY WAY TO HONOR HIS CITY AND STATE.

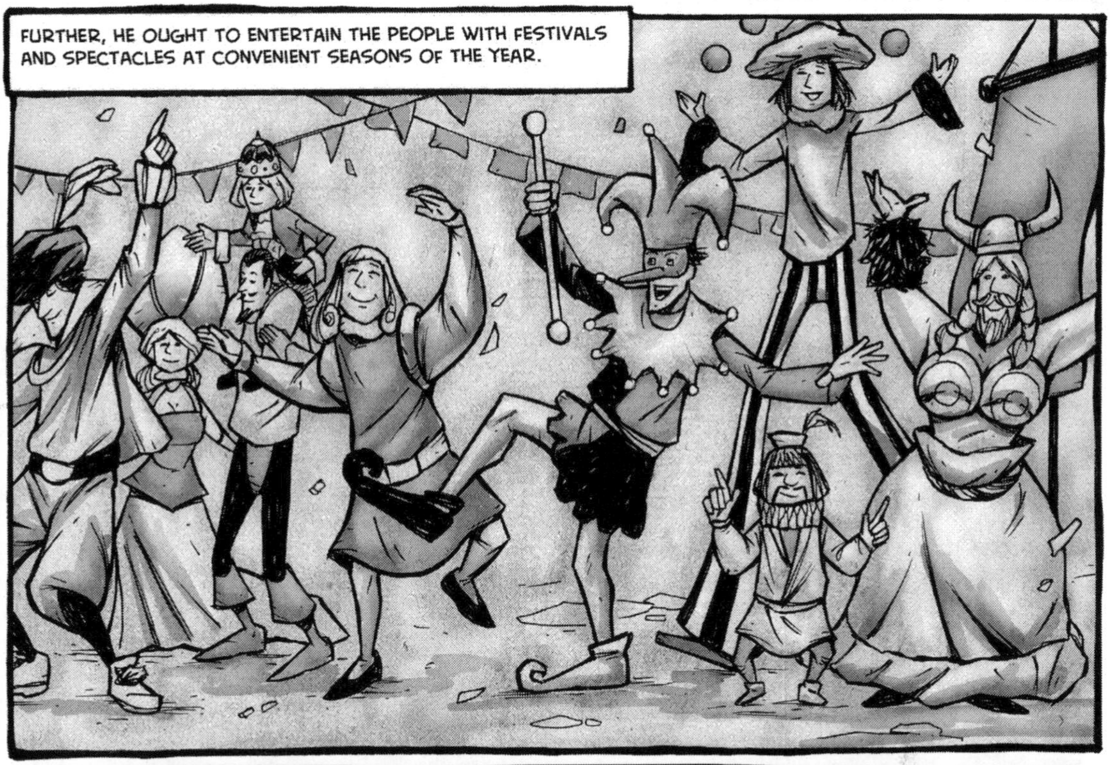
FURTHER, HE OUGHT TO ENTERTAIN THE PEOPLE WITH FESTIVALS AND SPECTACLES AT CONVENIENT SEASONS OF THE YEAR.

CONCERNING THE SECRETARIES OF PRINCES

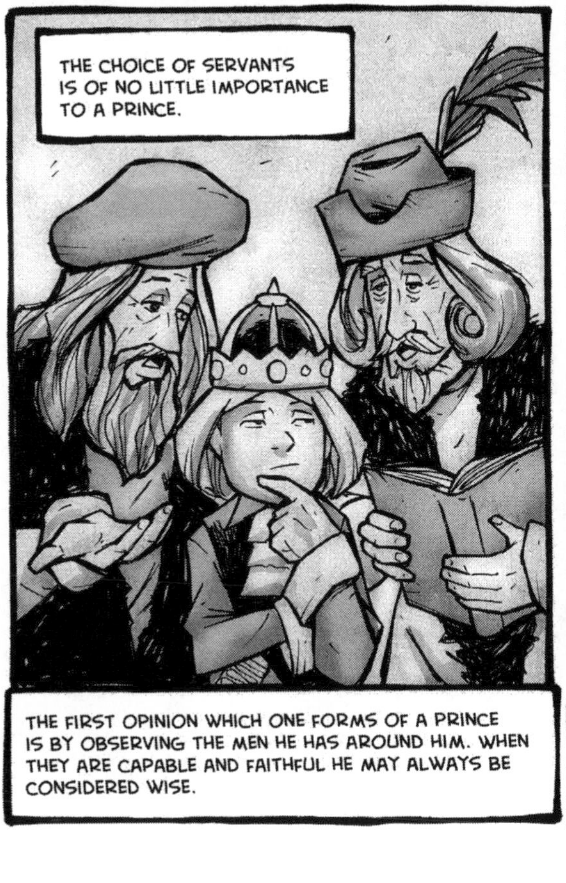
THE CHOICE OF SERVANTS IS OF NO LITTLE IMPORTANCE TO A PRINCE.
THE FIRST OPINION WHICH ONE FORMS OF A PRINCE IS BY OBSERVING THE MEN HE HAS AROUND HIM. WHEN THEY ARE CAPABLE AND FAITHFUL HE MAY ALWAYS BE CONSIDERED WISE.

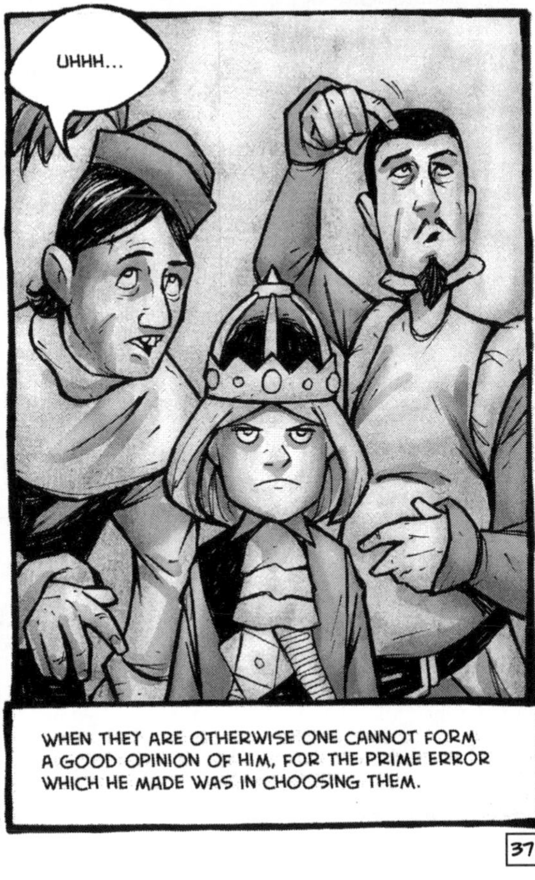
UHHH...
WHEN THEY ARE OTHERWISE ONE CANNOT FORM A GOOD OPINION OF HIM, FOR THE PRIME ERROR WHICH HE MADE WAS IN CHOOSING THEM.

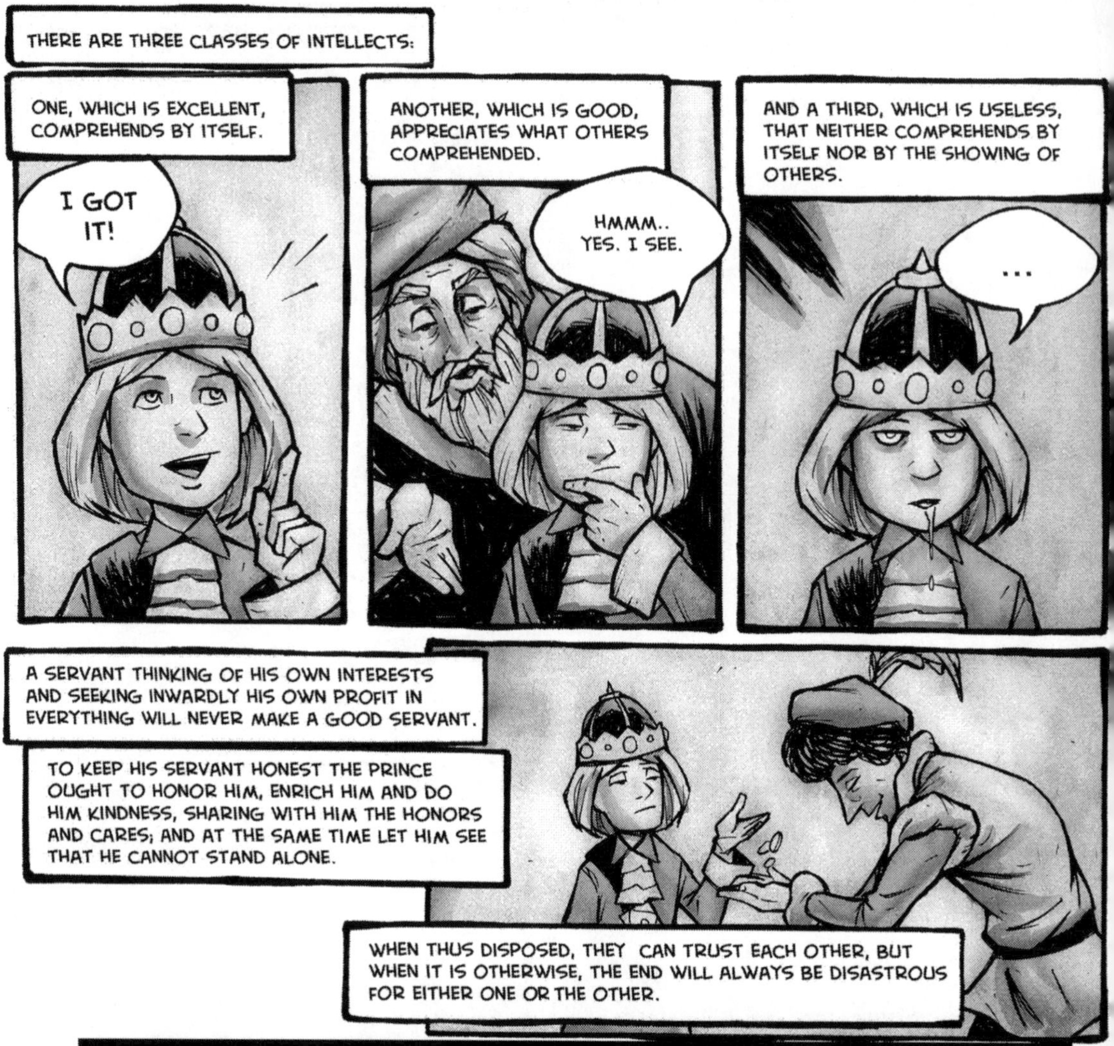
THERE ARE THREE CLASSES OF INTELLECTS:
ONE, WHICH IS EXCELLENT, COMPREHENDS BY ITSELF.
I GOT IT!
ANOTHER, WHICH IS GOOD, APPRECIATES WHAT OTHERS COMPREHENDED.
HMMM.. YES. I SEE.
AND A THIRD, WHICH IS USELESS, THAT NEITHER COMPREHENDS BY ITSELF NOR BY THE SHOWING OF OTHERS.
...
A SERVANT THINKING OF HIS OWN INTERESTS AND SEEKING INWARDLY HIS OWN PROFIT IN EVERYTHING WILL NEVER MAKE A GOOD SERVANT.
TO KEEP HIS SERVANT HONEST THE PRINCE OUGHT TO HONOR HIM, ENRICH HIM AND DO HIM KINDNESS, SHARING WITH HIM THE HONORS AND CARES; AND AT THE SAME TIME LET HIM SEE THAT HE CANNOT STAND ALONE.
WHEN THUS DISPOSED, THEY CAN TRUST EACH OTHER, BUT WHEN IT IS OTHERWISE, THE END WILL ALWAYS BE DISASTROUS FOR EITHER ONE OR THE OTHER.

HOW FLATTERERS SHOULD BE AVOIDED

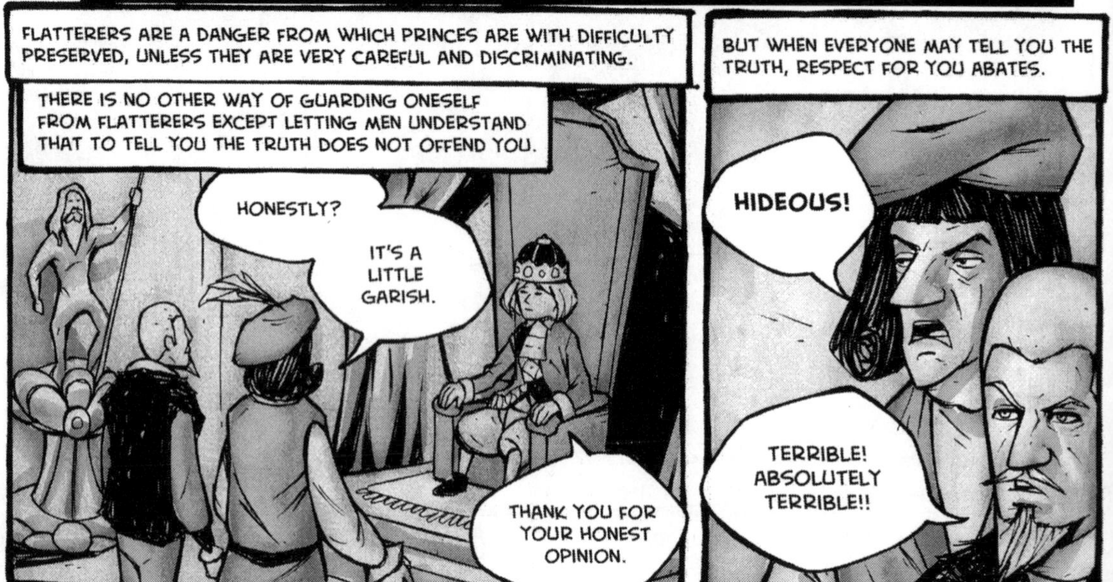
FLATTERERS ARE A DANGER FROM WHICH PRINCES ARE WITH DIFFICULTY PRESERVED, UNLESS THEY ARE VERY CAREFUL AND DISCRIMINATING.
THERE IS NO OTHER WAY OF GUARDING ONESELF FROM FLATTERERS EXCEPT LETTING MEN UNDERSTAND THAT TO TELL YOU THE TRUTH DOES NOT OFFEND YOU.
HONESTLY?
IT'S A LITTLE GARISH.
THANK YOU FOR YOUR HONEST OPINION.
BUT WHEN EVERYONE MAY TELL YOU THE TRUTH, RESPECT FOR YOU ABATES.
HIDEOUS!
TERRIBLE! ABSOLUTELY TERRIBLE!!

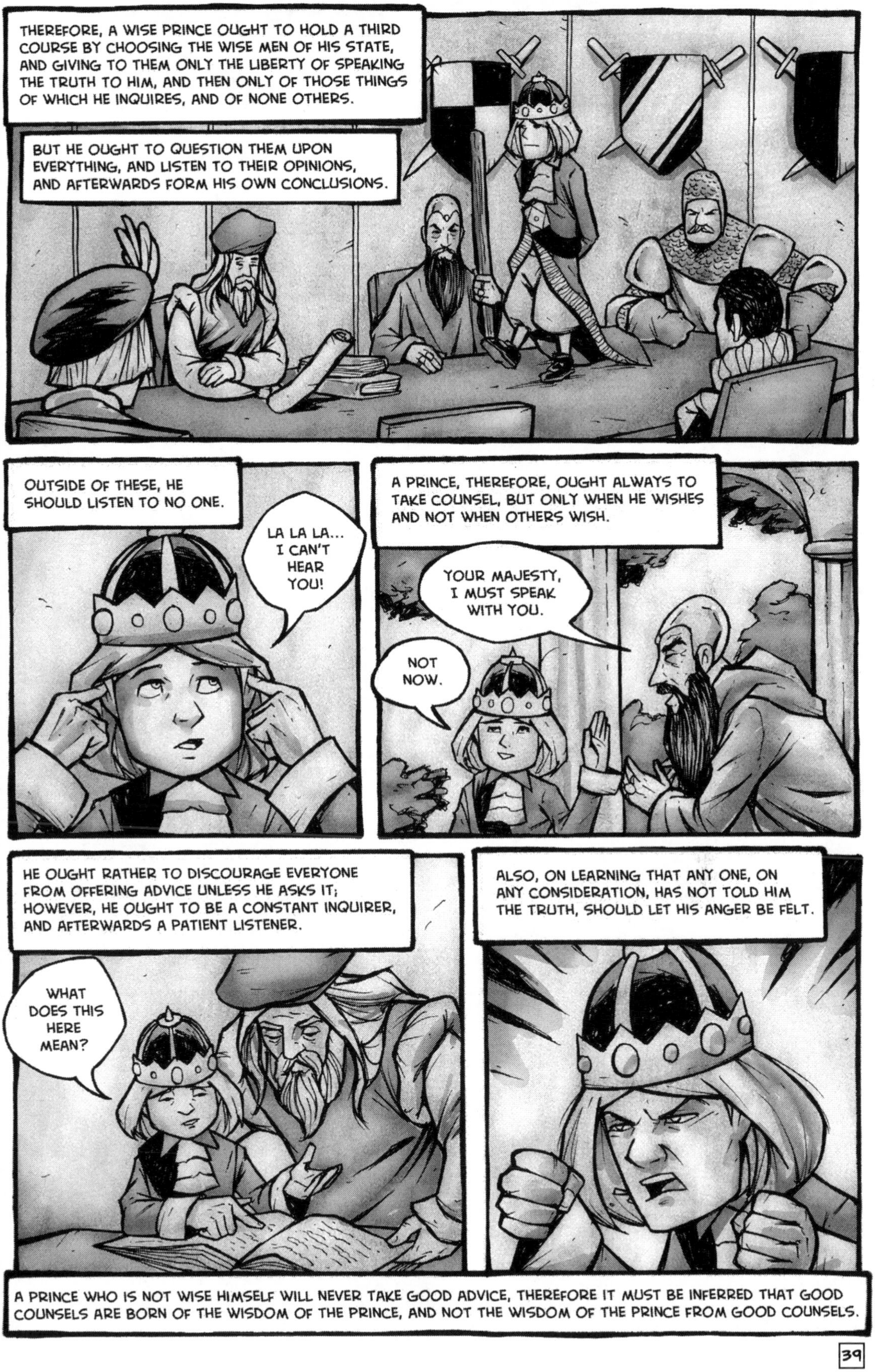
THEREFORE, A WISE PRINCE OUGHT TO HOLD A THIRD COURSE BY CHOOSING THE WISE MEN OF HIS STATE, AND GIVING TO THEM ONLY THE LIBERTY OF SPEAKING THE TRUTH TO HIM, AND THEN ONLY OF THOSE THINGS OF WHICH HE INQUIRES, AND OF NONE OTHERS.
BUT HE OUGHT TO QUESTION THEM UPON EVERYTHING, AND LISTEN TO THEIR OPINIONS, AND AFTERWARDS FORM HIS OWN CONCLUSIONS.
OUTSIDE OF THESE, HE SHOULD LISTEN TO NO ONE.
LA LA LA... I CAN'T HEAR YOU!
A PRINCE, THEREFORE, OUGHT ALWAYS TO TAKE COUNSEL, BUT ONLY WHEN HE WISHES AND NOT WHEN OTHERS WISH.
YOUR MAJESTY, I MUST SPEAK WITH YOU.
NOT NOW.
HE OUGHT RATHER TO DISCOURAGE EVERYONE FROM OFFERING ADVICE UNLESS HE ASKS IT; HOWEVER, HE OUGHT TO BE A CONSTANT INQUIRER, AND AFTERWARDS A PATIENT LISTENER.
WHAT DOES THIS HERE MEAN?
ALSO, ON LEARNING THAT ANY ONE, ON ANY CONSIDERATION, HAS NOT TOLD HIM THE TRUTH, SHOULD LET HIS ANGER BE FELT.
A PRINCE WHO IS NOT WISE HIMSELF WILL NEVER TAKE GOOD ADVICE, THEREFORE IT MUST BE INFERRED THAT GOOD COUNSELS ARE BORN OF THE WISDOM OF THE PRINCE, AND NOT THE WISDOM OF THE PRINCE FROM GOOD COUNSELS.

WHY THE PRINCES OF ITALY HAVE LOST THEIR STATES

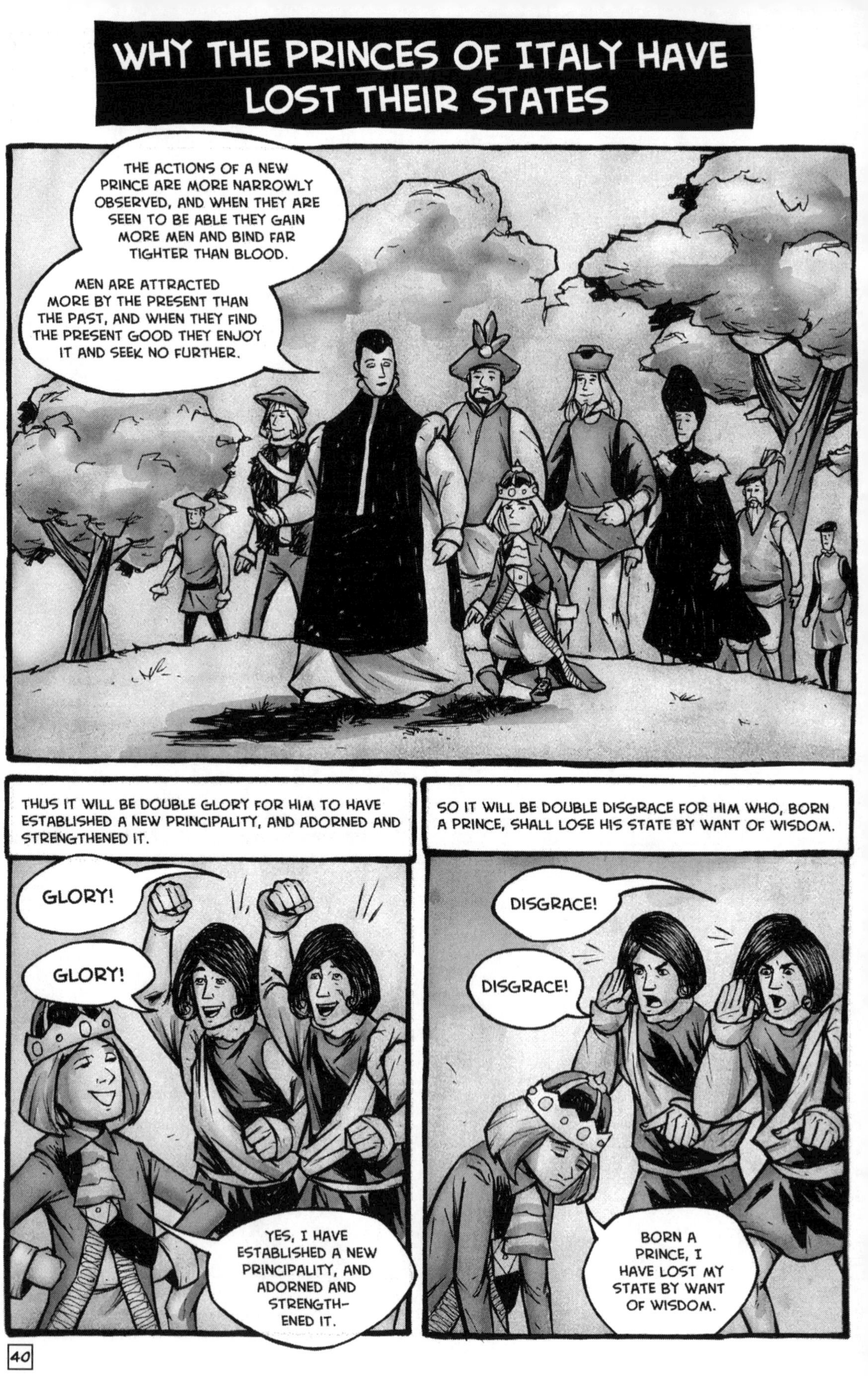

THE ACTIONS OF A NEW PRINCE ARE MORE NARROWLY OBSERVED, AND WHEN THEY ARE SEEN TO BE ABLE THEY GAIN MORE MEN AND BIND FAR TIGHTER THAN BLOOD.
MEN ARE ATTRACTED MORE BY THE PRESENT THAN THE PAST, AND WHEN THEY FIND THE PRESENT GOOD THEY ENJOY IT AND SEEK NO FURTHER.
THUS IT WILL BE DOUBLE GLORY FOR HIM TO HAVE ESTABLISHED A NEW PRINCIPALITY, AND ADORNED AND STRENGTHENED IT.
GLORY!
GLORY!
YES, I HAVE ESTABLISHED A NEW PRINCIPALITY, AND ADORNED AND STRENGTH-ENED IT.
SO IT WILL BE DOUBLE DISGRACE FOR HIM WHO, BORN A PRINCE, SHALL LOSE HIS STATE BY WANT OF WISDOM.
DISGRACE!
DISGRACE!
BORN A PRINCE, I HAVE LOST MY STATE BY WANT OF WISDOM.

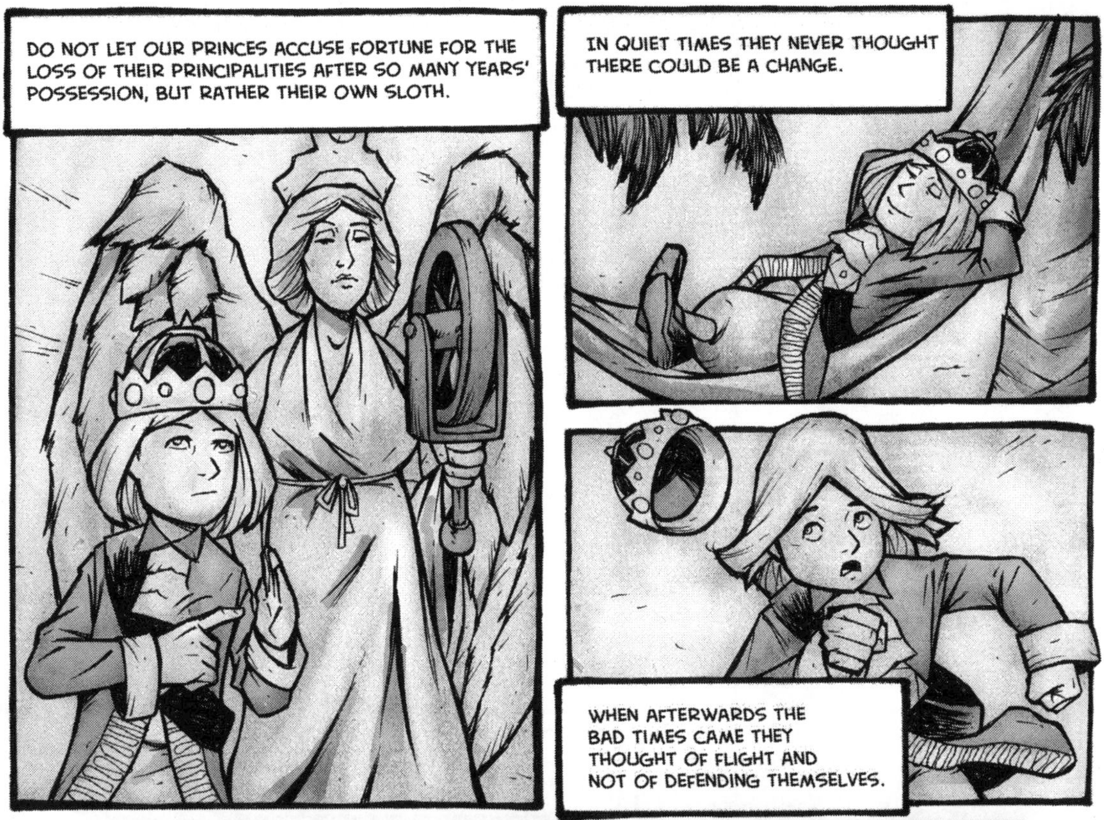
DO NOT LET OUR PRINCES ACCUSE FORTUNE FOR THE LOSS OF THEIR PRINCIPALITIES AFTER SO MANY YEARS' POSSESSION, BUT RATHER THEIR OWN SLOTH.
IN QUIET TIMES THEY NEVER THOUGHT THERE COULD BE A CHANGE.
WHEN AFTERWARDS THE BAD TIMES CAME THEY THOUGHT OF FLIGHT AND NOT OF DEFENDING THEMSELVES.

WHAT FORTUNE CAN EFFECT IN HUMAN AFFAIRS AND HOW TO WITHSTAND HER

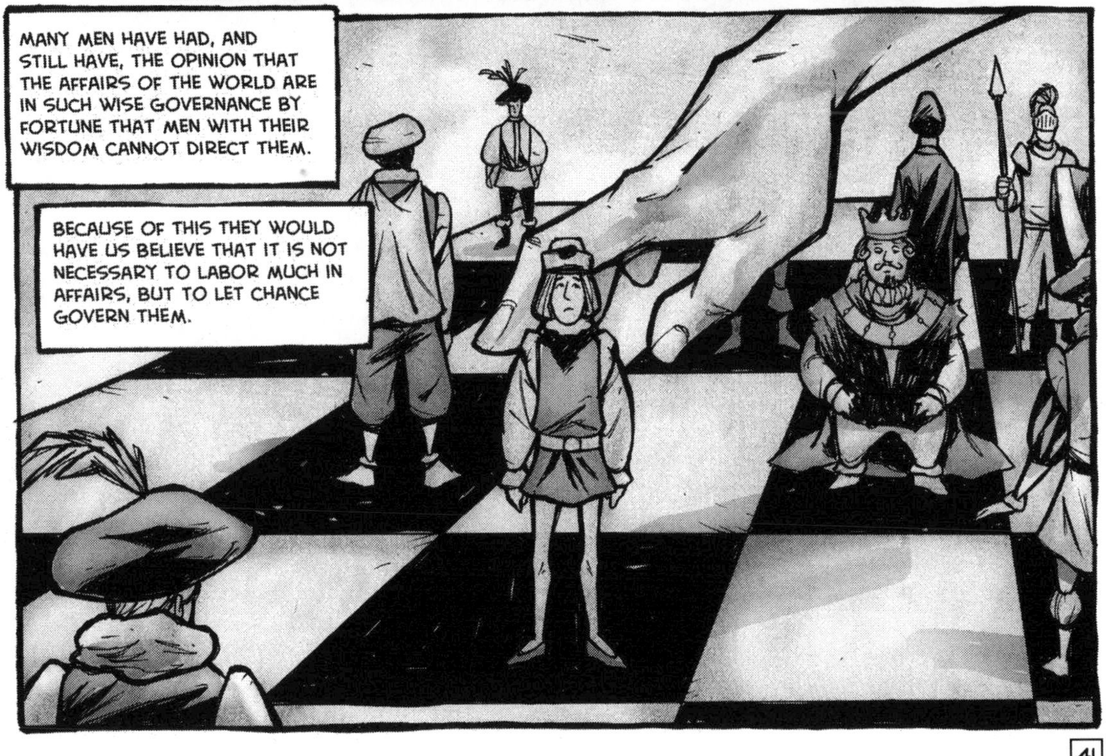
MANY MEN HAVE HAD, AND STILL HAVE, THE OPINION THAT THE AFFAIRS OF THE WORLD ARE IN SUCH WISE GOVERNANCE BY FORTUNE THAT MEN WITH THEIR WISDOM CANNOT DIRECT THEM.
BECAUSE OF THIS THEY WOULD HAVE US BELIEVE THAT IT IS NOT NECESSARY TO LABOR MUCH IN AFFAIRS, BUT TO LET CHANCE GOVERN THEM.

PONDERING OVER THIS, I AM IN SOME DEGREE INCLINED TO THEIR OPINION.

NEVERTHELESS, NOT TO EXTINGUISH OUR FREE WILL, I HOLD IT TO BE TRUE THAT FORTUNE IS THE ARBITER OF ONE-HALF OF OUR ACTIONS...

...BUT THAT SHE STILL LEAVES US TO DIRECT THE OTHER HALF.

A PRINCE MAY BE SEEN TO BE HAPPY TODAY...

THE PRINCE WHO RELIES ENTIRELY ON FORTUNE IS LOST WHEN IT CHANGES.

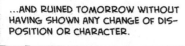

...AND RUINED TOMORROW WITHOUT HAVING SHOWN ANY CHANGE OF DISPOSITION OR CHARACTER.

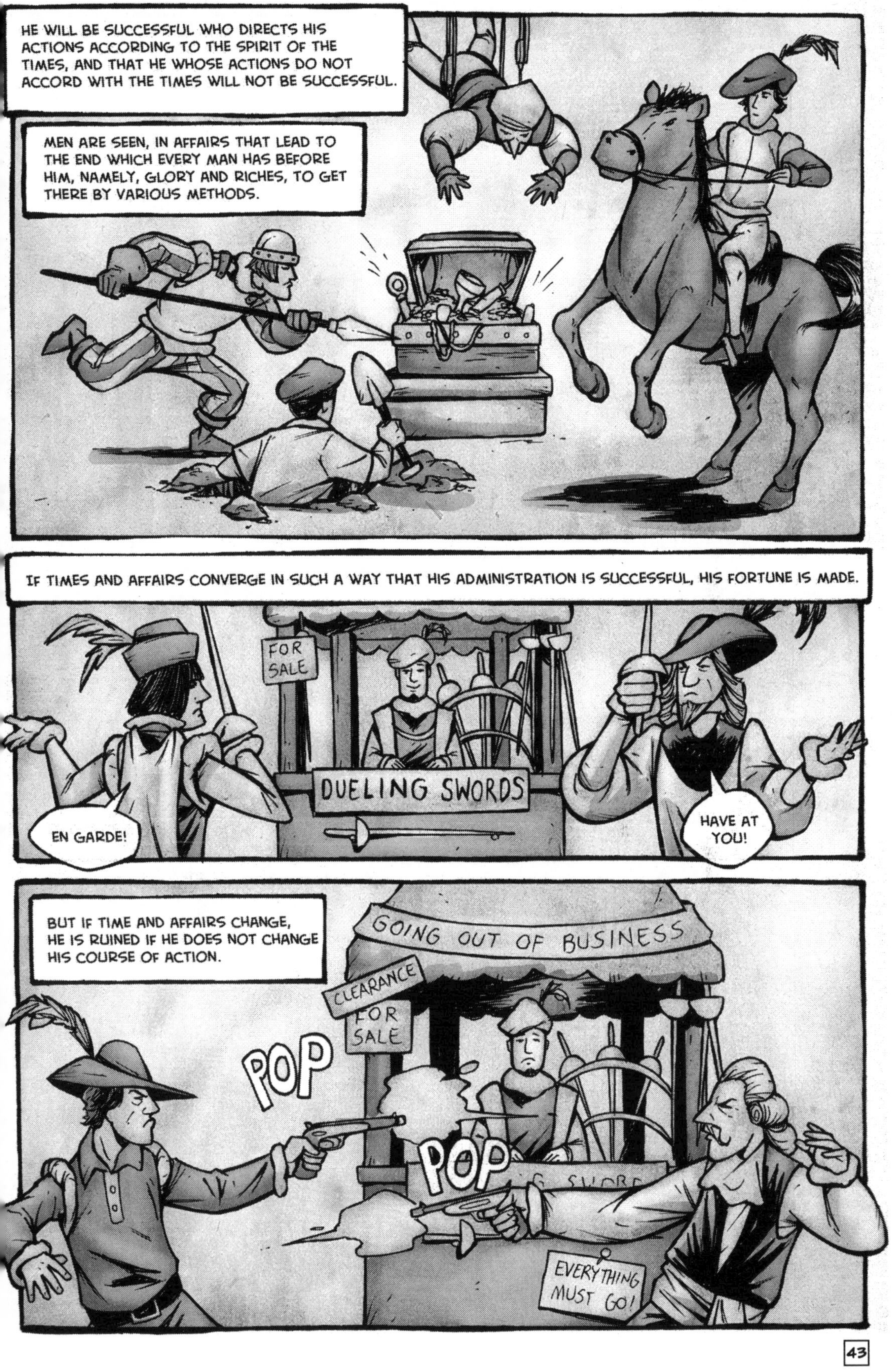
HE WILL BE SUCCESSFUL WHO DIRECTS HIS ACTIONS ACCORDING TO THE SPIRIT OF THE TIMES, AND THAT HE WHOSE ACTIONS DO NOT ACCORD WITH THE TIMES WILL NOT BE SUCCESSFUL.
MEN ARE SEEN, IN AFFAIRS THAT LEAD TO THE END WHICH EVERY MAN HAS BEFORE HIM, NAMELY, GLORY AND RICHES, TO GET THERE BY VARIOUS METHODS.
IF TIMES AND AFFAIRS CONVERGE IN SUCH A WAY THAT HIS ADMINISTRATION IS SUCCESSFUL, HIS FORTUNE IS MADE.
FOR SALE
DUELING SWORDS
EN GARDE!
HAVE AT YOU!
BUT IF TIME AND AFFAIRS CHANGE, HE IS RUINED IF HE DOES NOT CHANGE HIS COURSE OF ACTION.
GOING OUT OF BUSINESS
CLEARANCE
FOR SALE
POP
POP
EVERYTHING MUST GO!

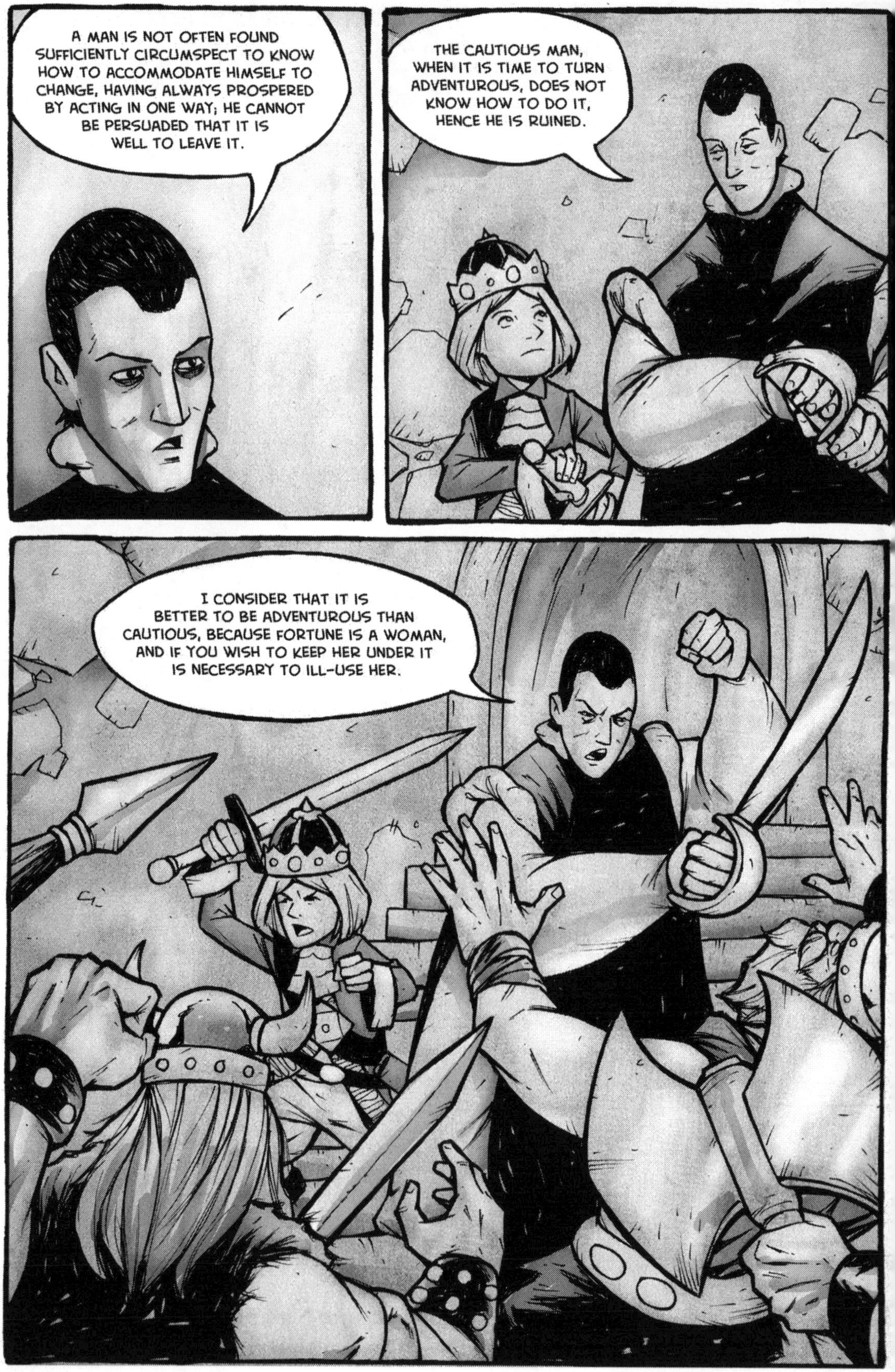
A MAN IS NOT OFTEN FOUND SUFFICIENTLY CIRCUMSPECT TO KNOW HOW TO ACCOMMODATE HIMSELF TO CHANGE, HAVING ALWAYS PROSPERED BY ACTING IN ONE WAY; HE CANNOT BE PERSUADED THAT IT IS WELL TO LEAVE IT.
THE CAUTIOUS MAN, WHEN IT IS TIME TO TURN ADVENTUROUS, DOES NOT KNOW HOW TO DO IT, HENCE HE IS RUINED.
I CONSIDER THAT IT IS BETTER TO BE ADVENTUROUS THAN CAUTIOUS, BECAUSE FORTUNE IS A WOMAN, AND IF YOU WISH TO KEEP HER UNDER IT IS NECESSARY TO ILL-USE HER.

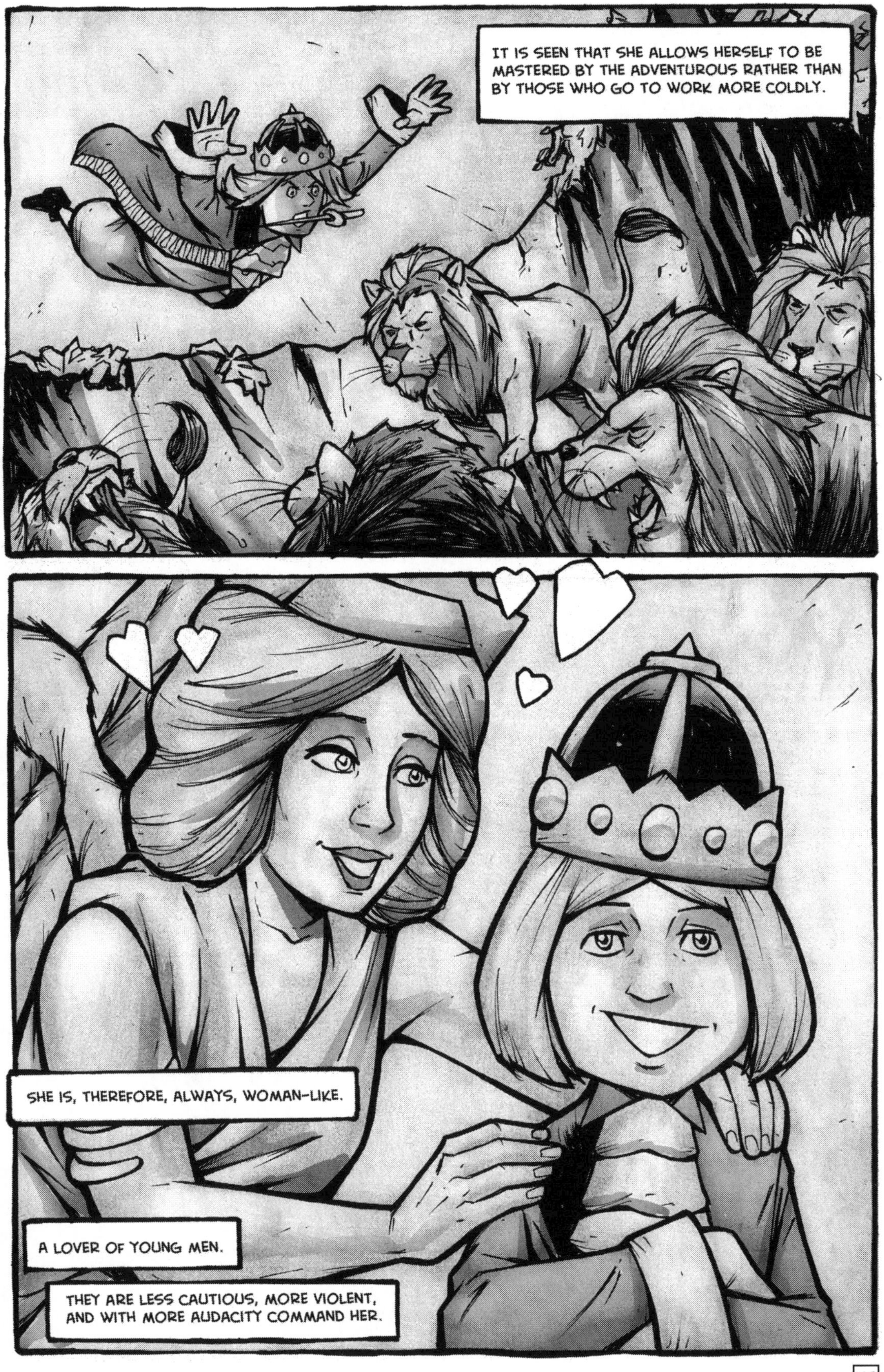
IT IS SEEN THAT SHE ALLOWS HERSELF TO BE MASTERED BY THE ADVENTUROUS RATHER THAN BY THOSE WHO GO TO WORK MORE COLDLY.
SHE IS, THEREFORE, ALWAYS, WOMAN-LIKE.
A LOVER OF YOUNG MEN.
THEY ARE LESS CAUTIOUS, MORE VIOLENT, AND WITH MORE AUDACITY COMMAND HER.

AN EXHORTATION TO LIBERATE ITALY FROM THE BARBARIANS

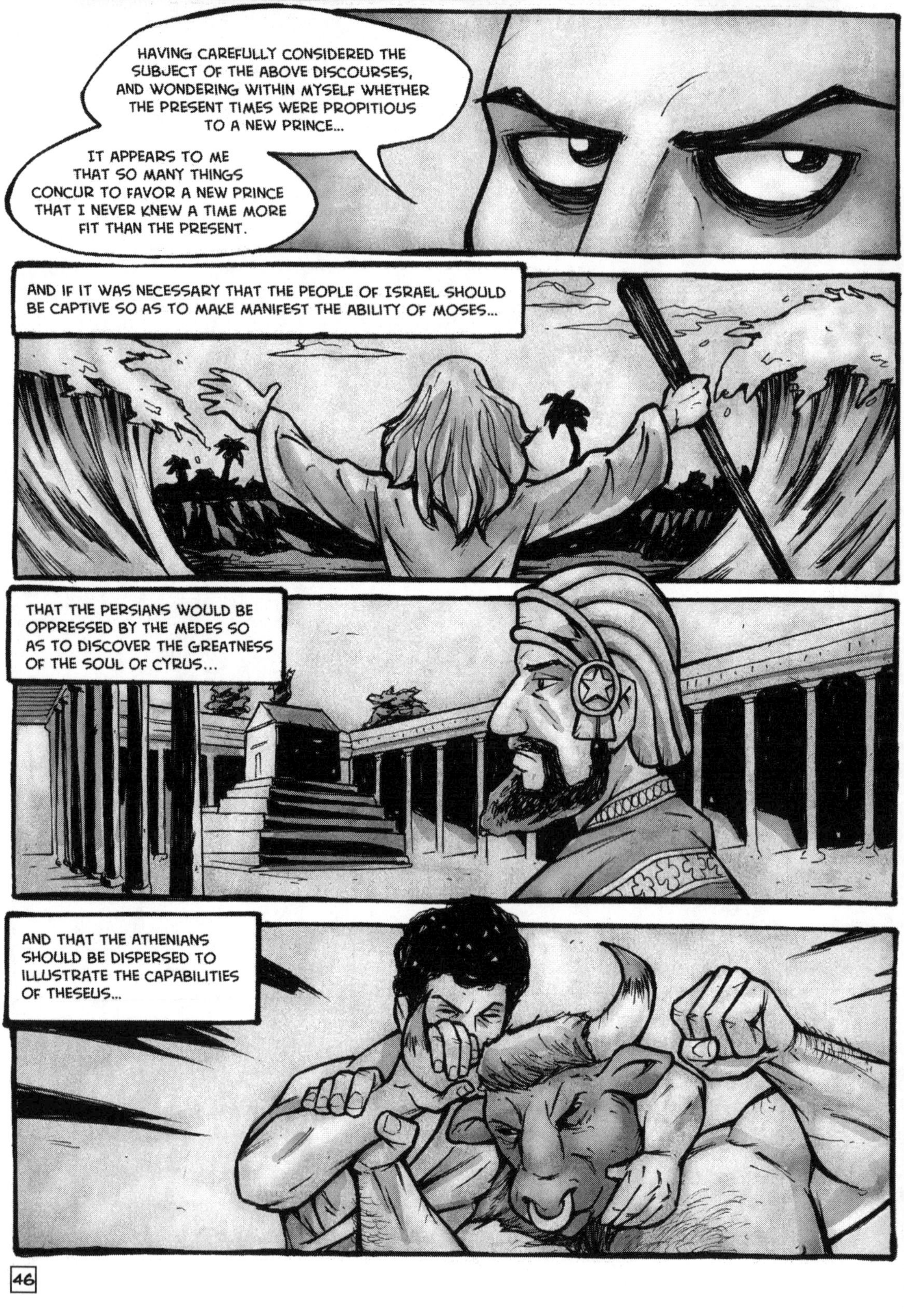
HAVING CAREFULLY CONSIDERED THE SUBJECT OF THE ABOVE DISCOURSES, AND WONDERING WITHIN MYSELF WHETHER THE PRESENT TIMES WERE PROPITIOUS TO A NEW PRINCE...
IT APPEARS TO ME THAT SO MANY THINGS CONCUR TO FAVOR A NEW PRINCE THAT I NEVER KNEW A TIME MORE FIT THAN THE PRESENT.
AND IF IT WAS NECESSARY THAT THE PEOPLE OF ISRAEL SHOULD BE CAPTIVE SO AS TO MAKE MANIFEST THE ABILITY OF MOSES...
THAT THE PERSIANS WOULD BE OPPRESSED BY THE MEDES SO AS TO DISCOVER THE GREATNESS OF THE SOUL OF CYRUS...
AND THAT THE ATHENIANS SHOULD BE DISPERSED TO ILLUSTRATE THE CAPABILITIES OF THESEUS...

THEN AT THE PRESENT TIME, IN ORDER TO DISCOVER THE VIRTUE OF AN ITALIAN SPIRIT, IT WAS NECESSARY THAT ITALY SHOULD BE REDUCED TO THE EXTREMITY THAT SHE IS NOW IN.

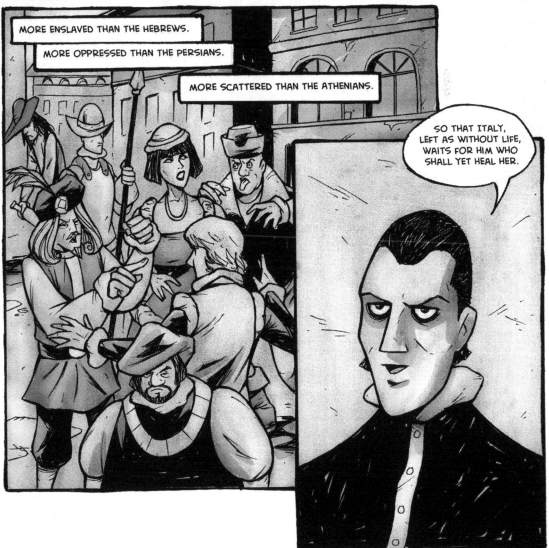

MORE ENSLAVED THAN THE HEBREWS.

MORE OPPRESSED THAN THE PERSIANS.

MORE SCATTERED THAN THE ATHENIANS.

SO THAT ITALY, LEFT AS WITHOUT LIFE, WAITS FOR HIM WHO SHALL YET HEAL HER.

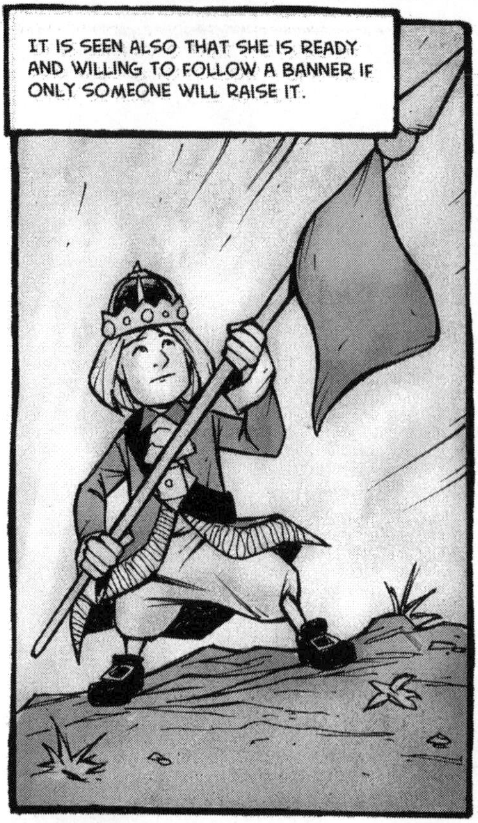
IT IS SEEN ALSO THAT SHE IS READY AND WILLING TO FOLLOW A BANNER IF ONLY SOMEONE WILL RAISE IT.

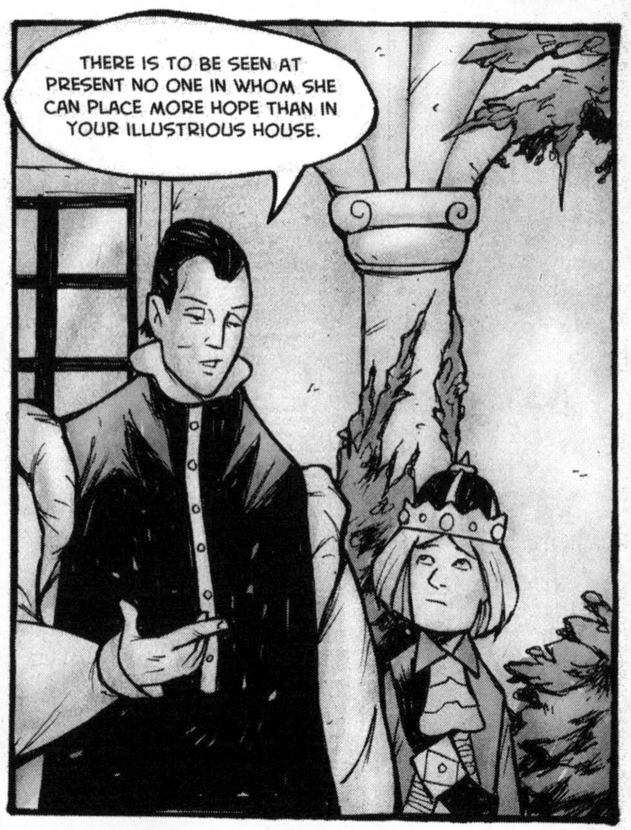
THERE IS TO BE SEEN AT PRESENT NO ONE IN WHOM SHE CAN PLACE MORE HOPE THAN IN YOUR ILLUSTRIOUS HOUSE.

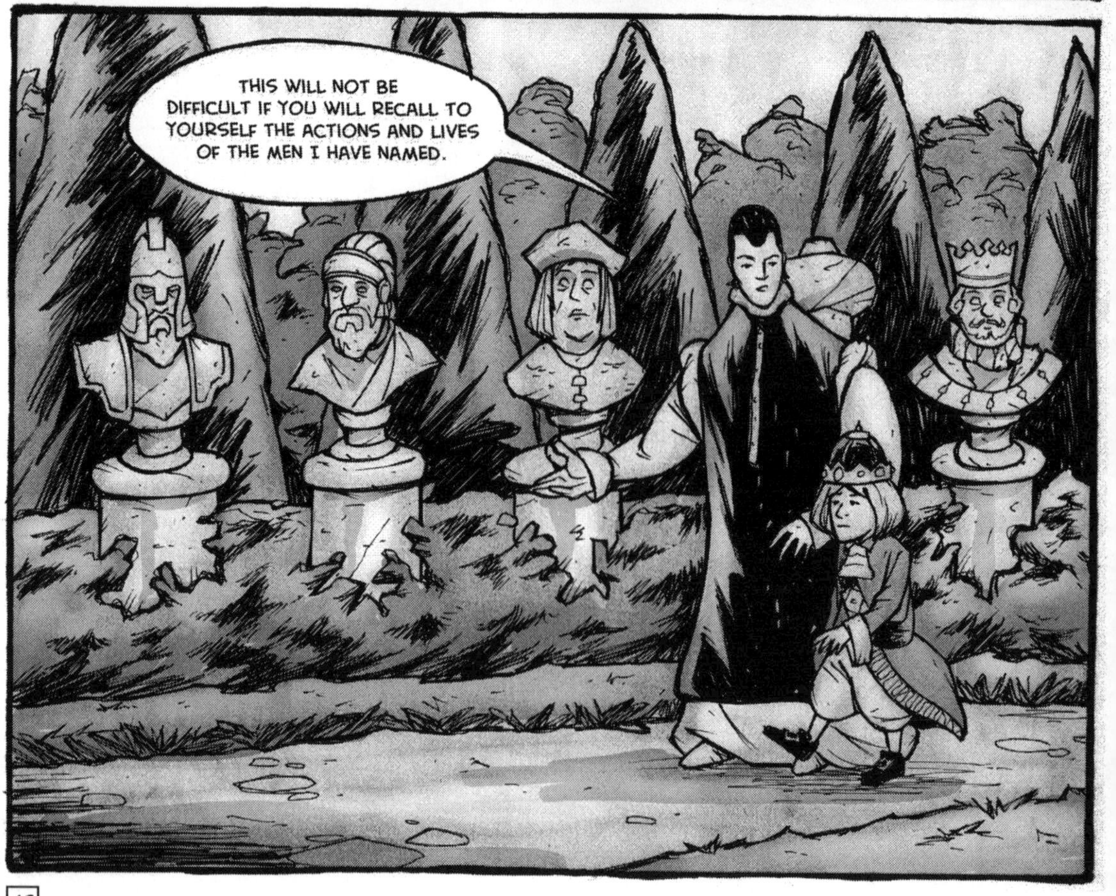
THIS WILL NOT BE DIFFICULT IF YOU WILL RECALL TO YOURSELF THE ACTIONS AND LIVES OF THE MEN I HAVE NAMED.

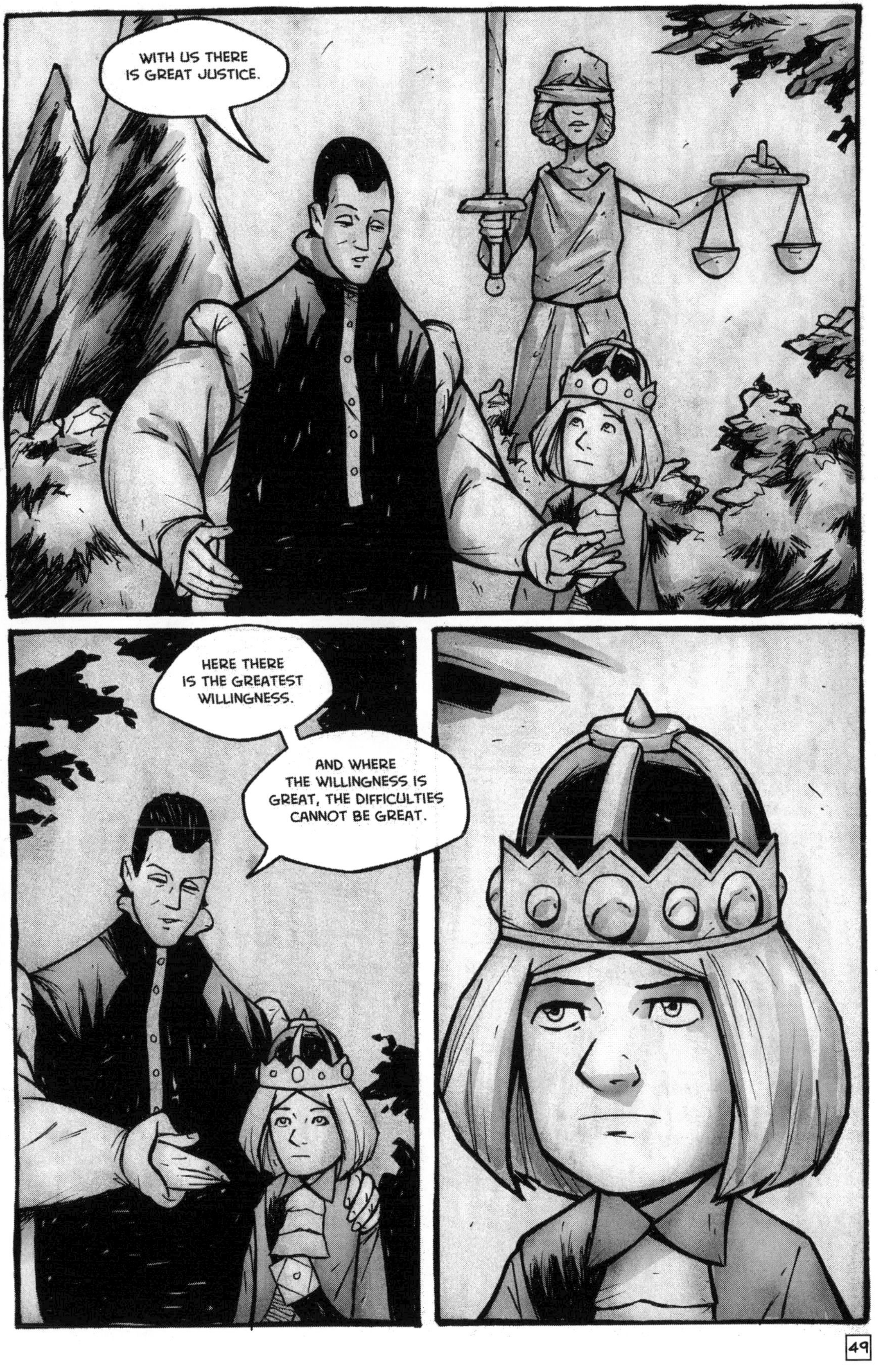
WITH US THERE IS GREAT JUSTICE.
HERE THERE IS THE GREATEST WILLINGNESS.
AND WHERE THE WILLINGNESS IS GREAT, THE DIFFICULTIES CANNOT BE GREAT.

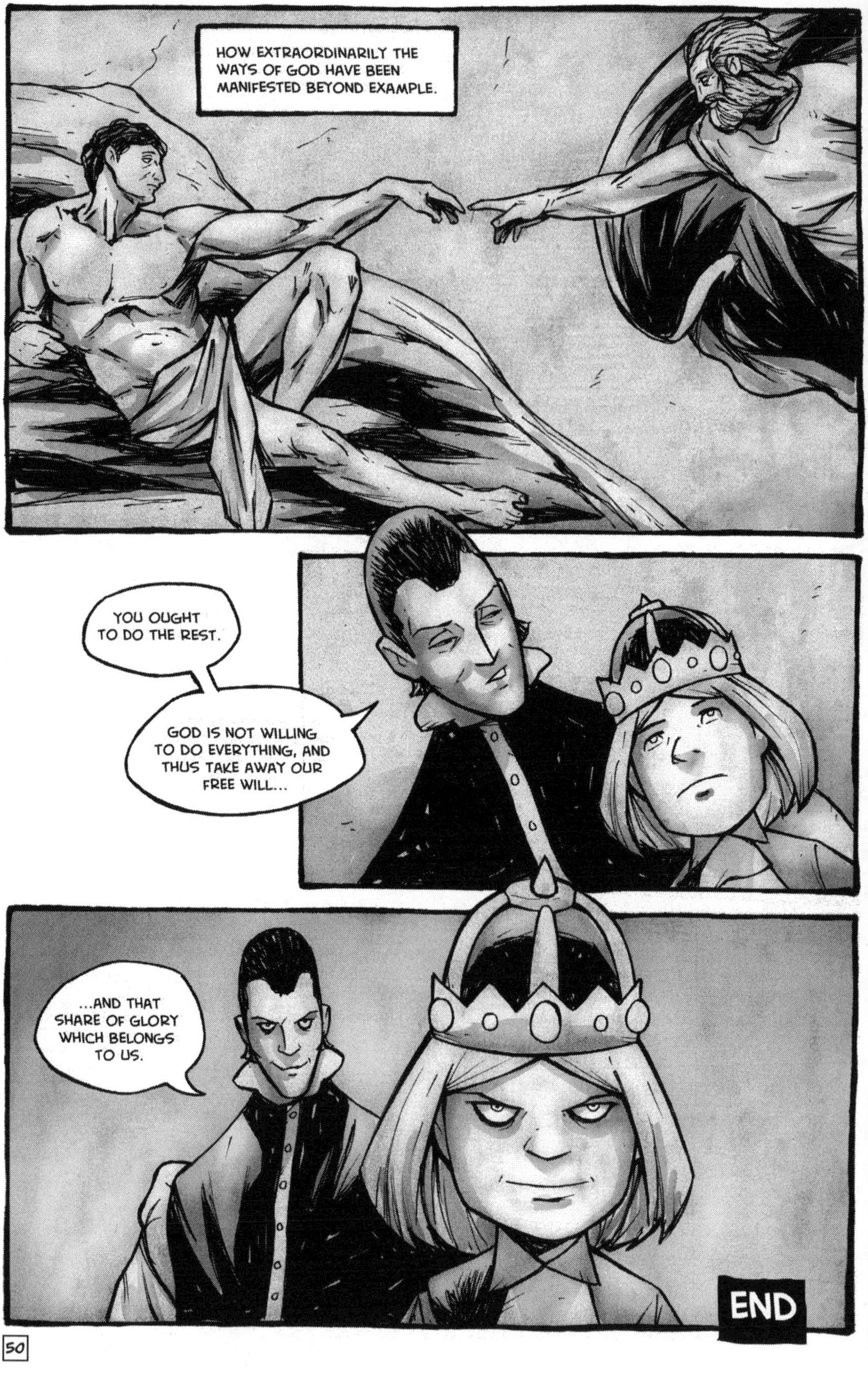
HOW EXTRAORDINARILY THE WAYS OF GOD HAVE BEEN MANIFESTED BEYOND EXAMPLE.
YOU OUGHT TO DO THE REST.
GOD IS NOT WILLING TO DO EVERYTHING, AND THUS TAKE AWAY OUR FREE WILL...
...AND THAT SHARE OF GLORY WHICH BELONGS TO US.
END

"I'M NOT INTERESTED IN PRESERVING THE
STATUS QUO; I WANT TO OVERTHROW IT."
- NICCOLO MACHIAVELLI

"If I were to teach high school humanities again, I would replace our textbook readings with Clester's adaptation of *The Prince* in a heartbeat—not as a parallel text for reluctant or struggling readers, but as the core text for students at all reading levels to get a first exposure to Machiavelli's ideas."

—**Dr. Sean Kottke**
Dean, Binda School of Education
The Robert B. Miller College

"Without oversimplifying the complexities of *The Prince*, Shane Chester has created a concise and accurate version of Machiavelli's work that will grab the attention of the high school reader. The whimsical artwork both clarifies and enhances the text and Chester's adaptation would be a valuable addition to any classroom library."

—**John C. Weaver, Ph.D.**
English Teacher, Williamsport Area High School

"The overall illustrative style is playful yet sophisticated, and certainly reverential to its source material, which Clester has clearly spent careful time considering. Machiavelli's character (true to his reputation) is portrayed with delicious ambiguity—as soon as a reader has let down his guard and accepted the philosopher's advice unquestioned, he is immediately bombarded on the next page with the character's dark, brooding eyes and coy half-smile, prompting instant reconsideration of what one has just read."

—**Nick Kreme**
Coordinator of Language Arts 6–12
Coordinator of Social Studies K–12
Columbia Public Schools

Niccolò di Bernardo dei Machiavelli (3 May 1469 – 21 June 1527) was an Italian philosopher and writer based in Florence during the Renaissance. He is one of the main founders of modern political science. He was a diplomat, political philosopher, playwright, and a civil servant of the Florentine Republic. He also wrote comedies, carnival songs, poetry, and some of the most well-known personal correspondence in the Italian language. His position in the regime of Florence as Secretary to the Second Chancery of the Republic of Florence lasted from 1498 to 1512, the period in which the de' Medici were not in power. The period when most of his well-known writing was done was after this, when they recovered power, and Machiavelli was removed from all functions.

"Shane Clester's graphic novel adaptation of Machiavelli's *The Prince* from Round Table Comics would be an excellent focus text for an interdisciplinary unit on the Italian Renaissance in a high school world literature course. Clester's illustrations provide openings for discussing many aspects of the Renaissance including advancements in architecture, exploration, and weaponry. The many allusions to Leonardo da Vinci could be the entry point into viewing and discussing Renaissance art, and the panel depicting festivals could be used to introduce Renaissance music and dance. In addition, Clester's portrayal of the prince from a variety of perspectives would provide opportunities for teachers to guide students in exploring issues of power."

—**Alisha M. White**
Graduate Research Assistant, Urban Literacy Clinic

"This totally belongs in social studies and language arts classrooms, both middle school and high school."

—**Dr. Katie Monnin**
Assistant Professor of Literacy
University of North Florida

"Shane Clester's graphic novel adaptation of Machiavelli's *The Prince*, proves to have inviting and stimulating imagery… I especially like how Clester uses quotes from Machiavelli himself, and introduces them in a casual and understandable way; this is a key part to teaching graphic novels. In addition, the use of traditional language makes the novel fun, yet challenging for those students who have never read anything outside of the modern novel."

—**Shannyn Stagner**
Secondary Ed.

At six years old, Shane Clester realized that most people aren't happy with their jobs. Even as he drew robots just to see if he could, he decided at that young age that he would turn his artistic play into work. As Shane grew older and studied the nuances of art, his initial excitement evolved into fascination. He was compelled by the replication of life through seemingly limited tools, and embarked on a quest to learn technical proficiency. In the early 2000s, Shane studied briefly under Jim Garrison, well-known for his art anatomy and technical skills. Shane then relocated from Arizona to California, where he learned a powerful lesson: You have to study to be an artist, and then you have to learn the business of being an artist.

Shane discovered that he needed to sell himself before he could sell a product. Over the course of the next several years, he broadened his portfolio to include youth-oriented art and comic books, and sourced clients by attending conferences and book fairs. Some of his clients have included leading comic book publisher IDW, Hasbro, Scholastic, Macmillan, and Times of London. Of his many projects, Shane is particularly proud of *Skate Farm: Volume 2*, a graphic novel he produced, and *Mi Barrio*, a comic book adaptation of Robert Renteria's *From the Barrio to the Board Room*.

The Prince Sketchbook

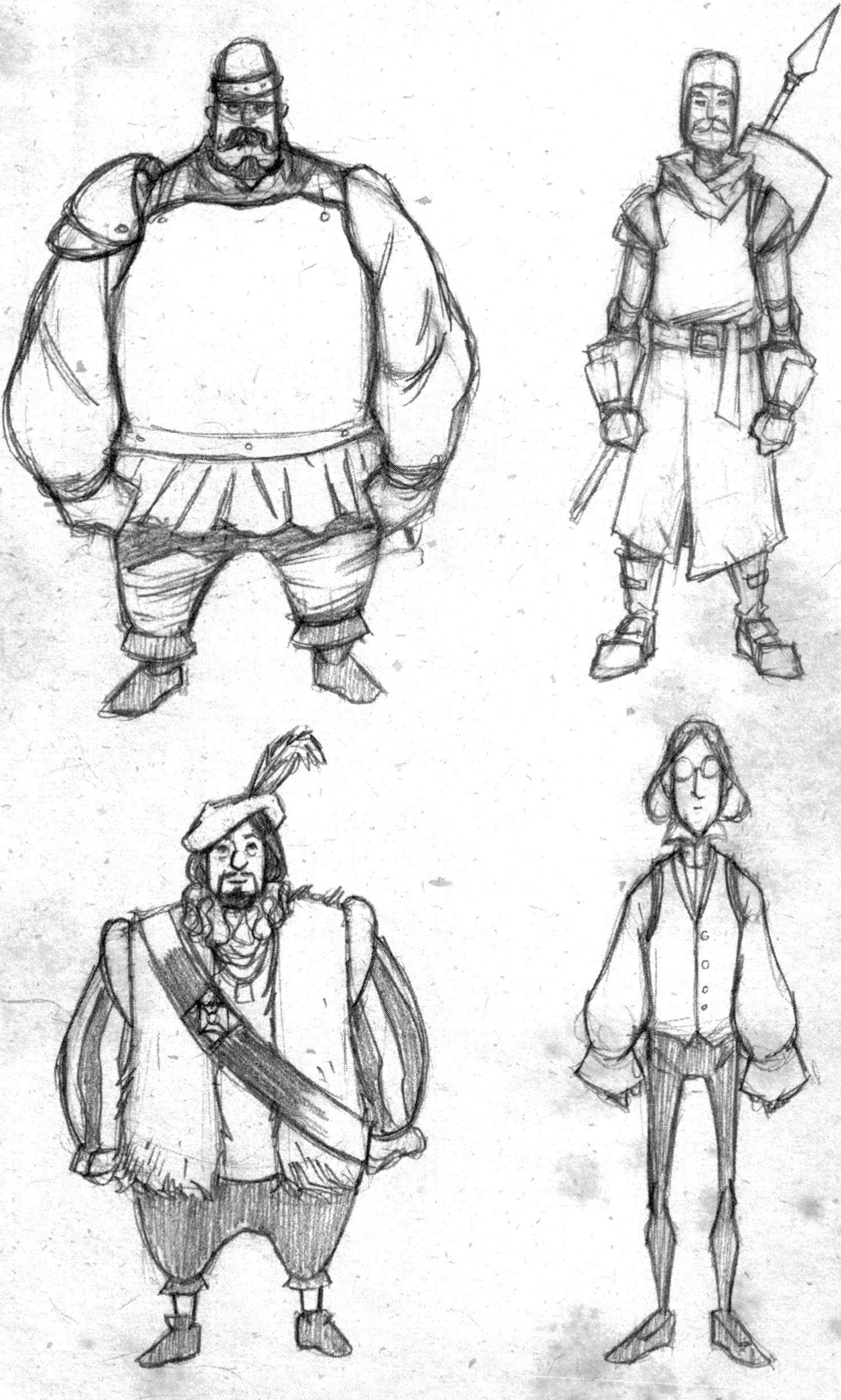

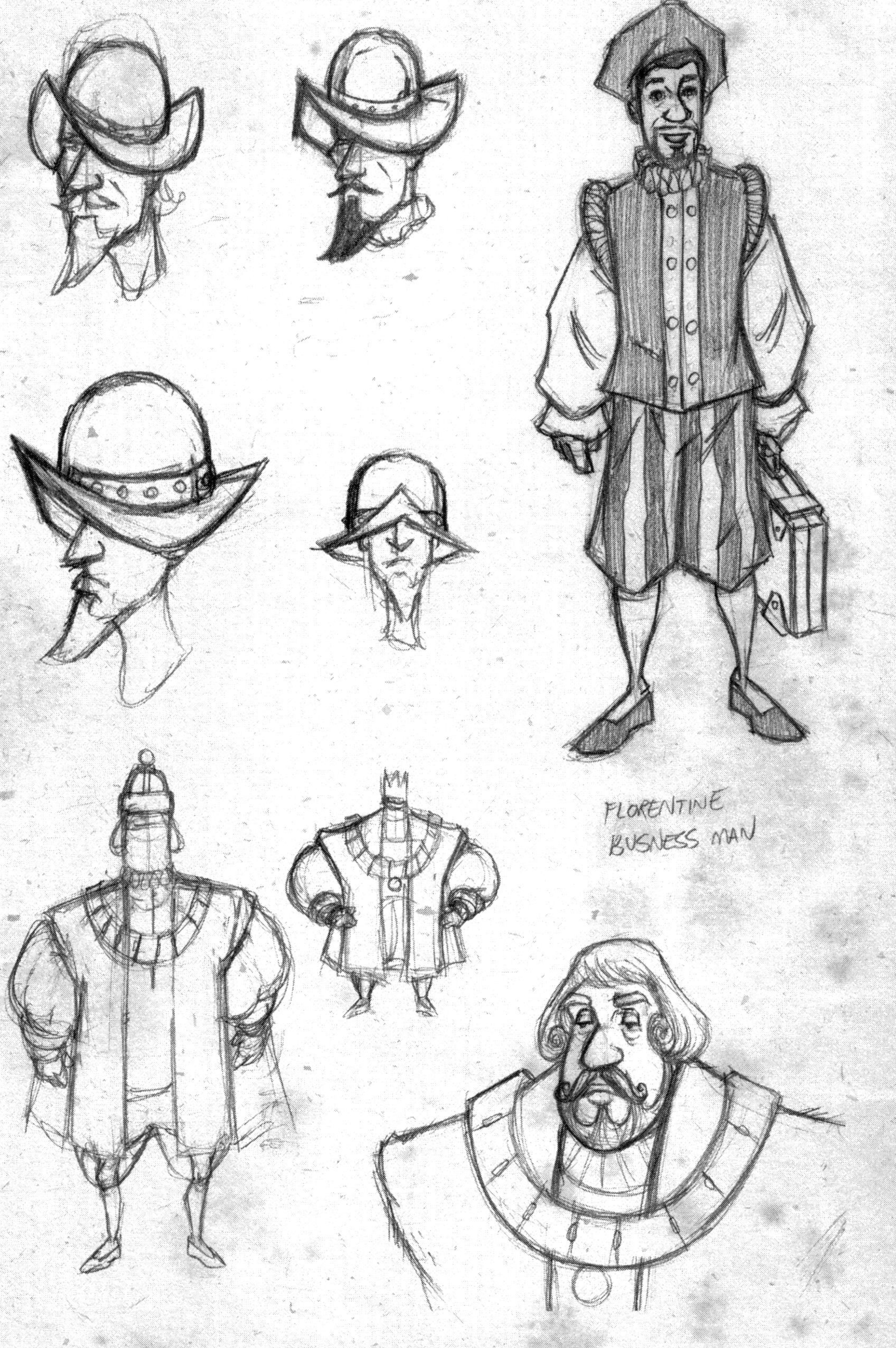
FLORENTINE
BUSNESS MAN

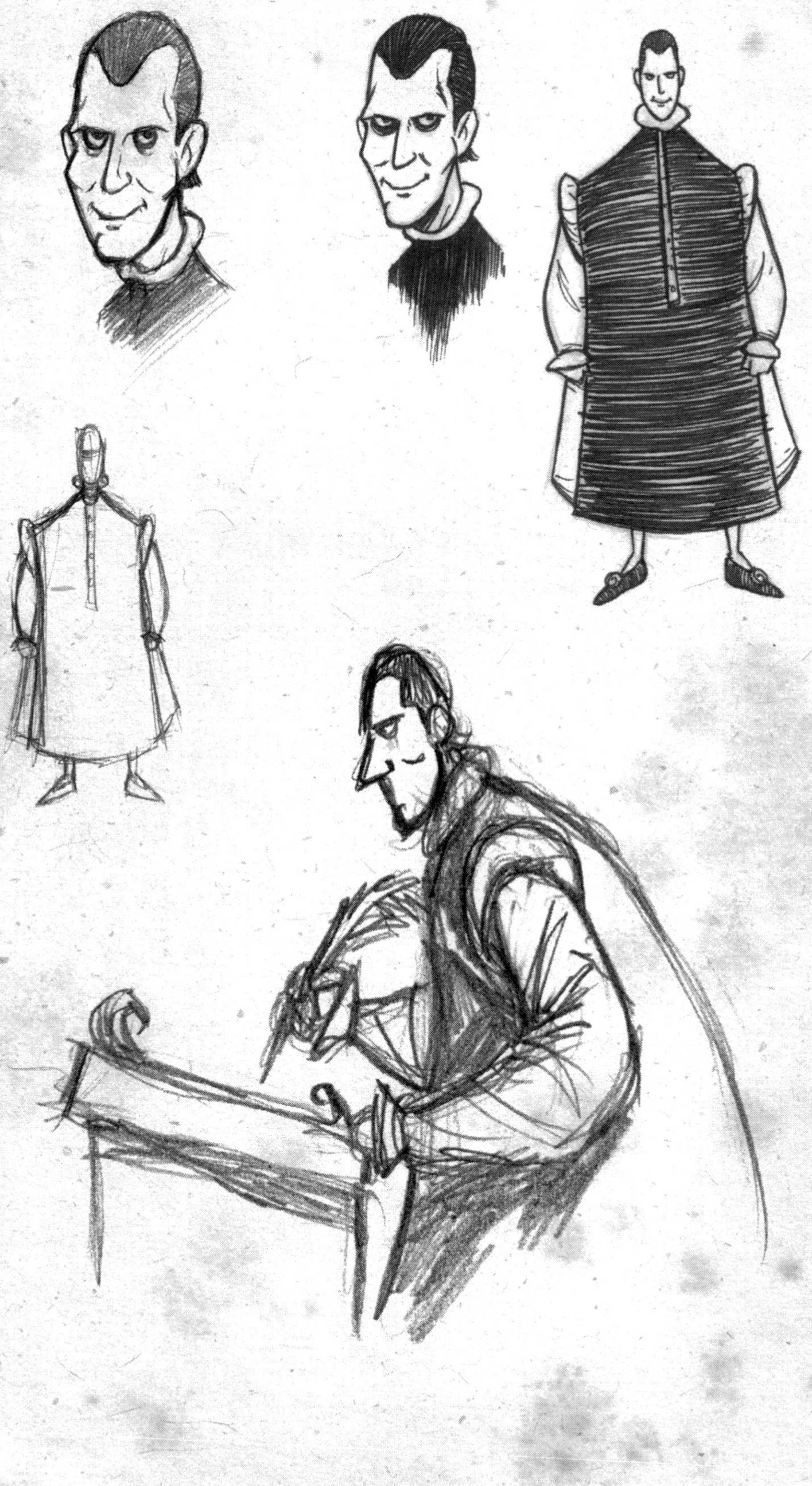

Cover Design Process

THIS IMAGE ↓ THIS RENDER →

COMING SOON FROM ROUND TABLE COMICS

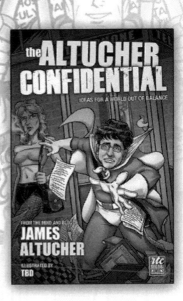

For more information visit:
www.roundtablecompanies.com

Follow us:
@RndTableCompanies

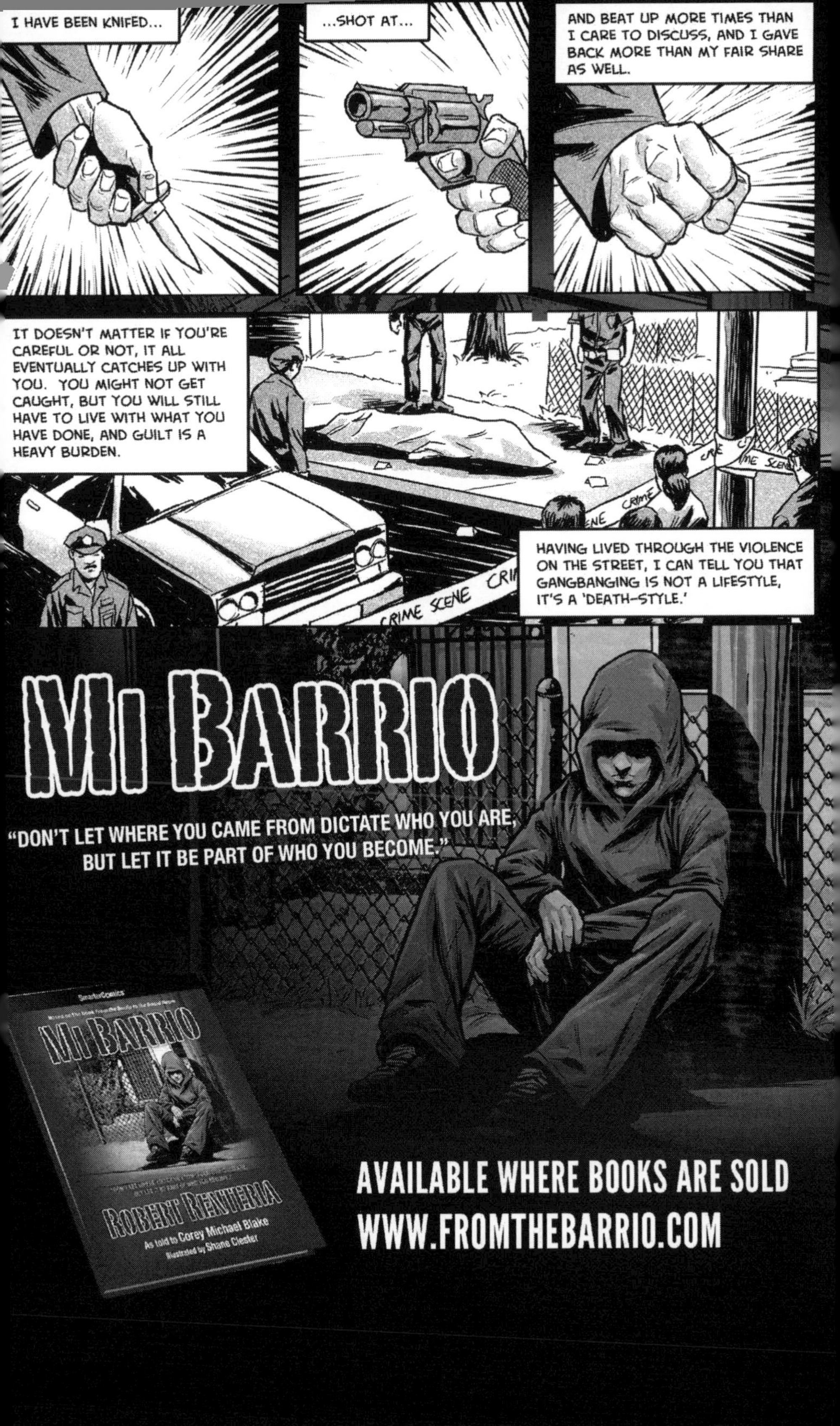
I HAVE BEEN KNIFED...
...SHOT AT...
AND BEAT UP MORE TIMES THAN I CARE TO DISCUSS, AND I GAVE BACK MORE THAN MY FAIR SHARE AS WELL.
IT DOESN'T MATTER IF YOU'RE CAREFUL OR NOT, IT ALL EVENTUALLY CATCHES UP WITH YOU. YOU MIGHT NOT GET CAUGHT, BUT YOU WILL STILL HAVE TO LIVE WITH WHAT YOU HAVE DONE, AND GUILT IS A HEAVY BURDEN.
CRIME SCENE
HAVING LIVED THROUGH THE VIOLENCE ON THE STREET, I CAN TELL YOU THAT GANGBANGING IS NOT A LIFESTYLE, IT'S A 'DEATH-STYLE.'
MI BARRIO
"DON'T LET WHERE YOU CAME FROM DICTATE WHO YOU ARE, BUT LET IT BE PART OF WHO YOU BECOME."
SmarterComics
MI BARRIO
ROBERT RENTERIA
As told to Corey Michael Blake
Illustrated by Shane Clester
AVAILABLE WHERE BOOKS ARE SOLD
WWW.FROMTHEBARRIO.COM

HOW SUCCESSFUL PEOPLE BECOME
EVEN MORE SUCCESSFUL

WHAT GOT YOU HERE WON'T GET YOU THERE

DISCOVER THE
20 WORKPLACE
HABITS THAT
YOU NEED TO
BREAK

MARSHALL GOLDSMITH

WITH MARK REITER

ILLUSTRATED BY
SHANE CLESTER

"The politics of Europe render it indispensably
necessary that we be one nation only,
firmly held together."

-Thomas Jefferson

THE UNITED STATES CONSTITUTION

A Graphic Novel

COMING SPRING 2012

rtc
ROUND TABLE
COMICS

@RndTableComics

Made in United States
Orlando, FL
09 March 2024

44578079R00046